A Bethnal Green
MEMOIR

A Bethnal Green
MEMOIR

Recollections of Life
in the 1930s–1950s

DEREK HOUGHTON

LARGE PRINT
Oxford

First published in Great Britain 2009
by
The History Press

Published in Large Print 2010 by ISIS Publishing Ltd.,
7 Centremead, Osney Mead, Oxford OX2 0ES
by arrangement with
The History Press

British Library Cataloguing in Publication Data
Houghton, Derek.
    A Bethnal Green memoir. – – (Reminiscence)
    1. Houghton, Derek - - Childhood and youth.
    2. Bethnal Green (London, England) - - Biography.
    3. Bethnal Green (London, England) - - History - -
    20th century.
    4. Bethnal Green (London, England) - - Social life
    and customs - - 20th century.
    5. Large type books.
    I. Title II. Series
    942.1'5084'092–dc22

ISBN 978–0–7531–9552–9 (hb)
ISBN 978–0–7531–9553–6 (pb)

Printed and bound in Great Britain by
T. J. International Ltd., Padstow, Cornwall

11721504

To my granddaughter Averil,
who has brought a ray of sunshine into our lives.

Contents

Acknowlegements

I am indebted to those who in the past suggested that I should write a book. To my wife Sheila; who was the source of encouragement, both in her advice and the long hours spent working on the manuscript. Carole Hamburger; who has been of tremendous help in reviewing and editing at each stage of writing. My sister Dawn, cousins Sheila, Brenda and Mavis; who furnished me with endless reminders of the past and provided photographs long since forgotten.

To write a book was a seed that has been lying dormant in the back of my mind for many years, ready to spring out. The prime reason for my writing is to record for my children, relatives, colleagues and friends how life really was in the East End's Bethnal Green.

Many have never comprehended the environment in which we grew up.

In the successful show and film *Fiddler on the Roof*, the main character, Tevye, played by Topol, looks up to heaven and speaks to God. "I know it's no great shame to be poor, on the other hand, it's no great honour either." Those words say a very great deal, especially to the likes of those like myself who grew up surrounded by poverty.

Finally I am eternally grateful to those families and

the boys and girls that I grew up with in St Peter's Avenue, and the people of Bethnal Green of that era. Without them there would have been no story to tell.

CHAPTER ONE

Our Street

There was once a street in Bethnal Green. How I wish that street were still there rather than having been replaced by uninspiring drab architecture, devoid of character and without soul; to be able to return once in a while, to stand in the street where I grew up. To look at the houses and the people who had lived in them, and to bring back the memories of my boyhood. This community, gone forever, was once bound by a common element — poverty. Everyone in that street knew everyone else; there was a "togetherness". It was like a village. It was a togetherness that grew even stronger when Hitler's Luftwaffe released their bombs on the East End of London.

Our street, St Peter's Avenue, was included in the council's slum clearance proposals in the five years leading up to 1965. At the stroke of a pen, faceless officials sitting in the town hall's council chamber concluded that our street was to be demolished forever; its community spirit broken and its residents scattered to the four corners of Tower Hamlets, to dwell in cold, grey, concrete, monolithic jungles. The likelihood of seeing the people whom I grew up with ever again was slim.

Many of the streets that were to remain could not compare with St Peter's Avenue. It was bounded by Hackney Road to the north, which in 1587 was referred to as the highway from Shoreditch to Mare Street. Old Bethnal Green Road lay to the south, which in 1538 was named Cocks Lane. In 1642 it became Rogues Lane, and in 1717, Whores Lane. It finally became acceptable when it was named Old Bethnal Green Road. Warner Place lay to the west and Mansford Street to the east.

It was a street like many others in Bethnal Green, a street of terraced houses, and the larger houses at the top had at one time of their lives housed the gentry. The basements were kitchens and sculleries, while the top of the houses acted as servant's quarters. They had been very grand in their day.

Others graduated to even smaller houses, as you walked from Hackney Road. Two-thirds of the houses in the street were built in a uniform fashion of three upper rooms. The upper front room, with two large windows looking out on to the street, had two small balconies with a decorative wrought iron surround, large enough to accommodate your bottom and watch any parade that might be passing by! There were three rooms on the lower ground floor. These included a scullery, and a small garden, and yard with an outside toilet. The luxury of having a bathroom was totally unknown. No one owned their home, they were all rented. The very thought of buying your own house was never considered, it would have been like placing a millstone around your neck. Besides, very few were in a position to qualify for a mortgage even if they had wanted to. Unemployment was high, jobs were scarce, and we were in a depression.

There was something very special about our street; I could never quite put my finger on it, never really understanding why it felt so special, but it did. To my mind, it was a cut above the surrounding streets, as it was never scruffy or run down, nor did it have an air of poverty about it. What is it with a street that becomes part of you, that you feel it and breathe it?

Poverty was forever there. Getting through each day to see that there was a meal on the table to feed the family. Scheming and scratching to make ends meet, sharing the despair with neighbours in the same inescapable position as you. Poverty compelled you to take roads you did not want to travel down, having no option but to do so if it meant survival. Under these conditions, Bethnal Green was a perfect breeding ground for those who had higher aspirations. It was like the embryo for the criminal, the fighter, and for those seeking a better way of life, all trying to find a way out.

The 1930s was a decade of depression. Unemployment was at its peak, and there were many people in the East End who resorted to crime to make ends meet. Each week the local rag, *The Hackney Gazette*, would publish the court cases. The findings of the courts were much harsher then in meting out sentences and punishment to the guilty offenders. Robbery with violence was considered a very serious crime. On

3

21 July 1933, Frank Muir, aged twenty, was sentenced to four years' penal servitude, plus eighteen strokes of the cat-of-nine-tails for robbing women with violence. The counterfeiting of £1 notes, half crowns, florins and shillings abounded. In November 1934, one man was found passing forged £1 notes at Clapton Dog Stadium and was sentenced to seven years' penal servitude. In the same year, James Sims of 36 Nelson Street was found to be in possession of nine counterfeit florins and was sentenced to two years' penal servitude. Counterfeiting had become quite rampant during those years.

To understand the circumstances and conditions, one has to look into the history of Bethnal Green. Poverty had been in and around Bethnal Green for a very long time; overcrowding was caused by poverty. Since the poor could not afford more spacious abodes they needed to stay close to their work. In the late 1880s the largest category of the population was "comfortable" with a fairly good wage coming in. These were mainly craftsmen in the furniture trade. Bethnal Green had the highest percentage of poor and very poor, mostly labourers and people underemployed in the furniture and dress trades. The "comfortable" artisans and clerks lived around Victoria Park.

In 1881, 872 out of a population of 129,000 people in Bethnal Green were Irish and 925 foreign-born. Foreign immigrants formed a minute percentage of the population. Mostly born in Germany, Poland, and Russia, they were the poor Jews who had fled the pogroms and whose concentration made them stand out more than their numbers merited. By 1899, Jews formed at least 95 per cent of the population south of Mare Street, and almost 80 per cent in Brick Lane. The ghetto, full of synagogues, backroom factories, and little grocery stores reeking of pickled herring, garlic sausage and onion bread, was occupied by alien people speaking a strange language. The smell of sweat, overcrowding, and high rents were associated with Jews, as victims and sometimes as perpetrators. Some Jews were middle class and invested in property which they rack rented. Anti-Jewish feeling, fuelled by the resentment of slum dwellers, expelled in the clearances, ignited against the landlords in 1898.

The liberal Jewish establishment of the United Synagogue, including Sir Samuel Montagu and the Rothschilds, understood the danger of the unarticulated alien. They opposed the sweating system and rack renting. It resulted in them founding the Four Per Cent Industrial Dwellings Company to provide homes for Jewish artisans. One benefit of the Jewish settlement that found agreement, acknowledged by their opponents, the missioners, was the declining incidence of drunkenness, and possibly because of that, the decline in infant mortality.

The distended numbers of Jews aggravated poverty and crowding. By 1901 there was an overall concentration in Bethnal Green of 170 people per acre. The number of houses reached 17,283 in 1881 and 17,354 in 1891; a density of twenty-three houses per acre, after which numbers seem to decrease, to 14,848 in 1901 and 13,649 in 1911. Most people (76 per cent in 1901 and 79 per cent in 1911) lived in tenements

5

with fewer than five rooms, with nearly a third of those in just two rooms. In the 1880s there were old houses where the upper room, once used for weaving, had been portioned in two or three rooms for two families, with another family on each floor. Overcrowding was made worse by the loss of gardens to workshops and warehouses, although sanitation improved.

One of my earliest recollections of poverty which had a long lasting effect was the eviction of a husband and wife from their home because they were unable to pay their rent. Neighbours stood around their furniture, stacked at the curbside, in total silence with a feeling of helplessness at seeing the contents of their home put out on the street. The poor woman was sobbing her heart out, clutching at her children's hands, her children too young to understand their parents' plight. The neighbouring women standing around were sharing her misery and crying too. It was a profoundly unforgettable experience.

In its better days, one of St Peter's Street's most celebrated residents was Wilkie Collins, the nineteenth-century author best known for *The Women in White*, which many years later would be made into a musical by Andrew Lloyd Webber. He also wrote one of the first detective novels, *The Moonstone*. A very successful author, he was a great friend of Charles Dickens.

Further down the road at No. 70 resided Horatio Bottomley. In 1888 he founded the *Financial Times* and was its first chairman. In 1906 he established the patriotic journal *John Bull*, and he was also elected Liberal MP for the Borough of Hackney. Bottomley's politics earned him a reputation as a populist, but his financial strategies meant he was seen as a common swindler by many. He was later charged with fraud and mismanagement, and was sentenced to seven years' imprisonment and expelled from Parliament. He died in penury in 1933.

It was commonplace for many of the homes to have two families living in them. Normally when a son or daughter married, they would move in with their parents and occupy the upper part of the house. If children came along, the house would accommodate six to seven people, if not more. The first floor landing was utilized as a kitchen, having a gas stove installed, and the only toilet for both families would be outside in the yard.

The women in our street generally wore a crossover apron, and in the summer months it was often the only outer garment worn. There were two elderly ladies down the street, very prim and proper who always wore mop caps, and seemed to belong to another age. Everyone knew them as the "old maids". Whenever you passed their house, you would find them cleaning, dusting and polishing. Most women took pride in their homes, both inside and out. Doorsteps were hand rubbed in either white or green hearthstone. Some steps looked decidedly smarter where red cardinal polish was applied, if they could afford it that is.

The pavement immediately outside the homes was washed and scrubbed with birch brooms. Door knockers, doorknobs, letter boxes, and foot gratings were polished. Some knockers and door handles were black, and, like the foot grating, they would be polished with Zebo, a black graphite polish. Others were made of brass, and seldom would you see any brass door furniture tarnished. Many front doors were artificially grained to give the appearance of a more expensive type of wood. "Japanning" and "Graining" have since become a lost art; you rarely see this type of work anymore.

Just two or three years before the outbreak of the war, the name of our street was changed from St Peter's Street to St Peter's Avenue. Smart, white enameled street signs in black lettering, with the Borough of Bethnal Green lettered in red, were placed above the existing old street signs. It was almost like feeling we had "arrived" and had been given class status!

I was too young at the time to give any thought as to why the name was changed, but later came to realise that we did after all have trees in our street, not very mature ones, but trees nevertheless! This had probably given us the entitlement of calling ourselves an "Avenue". It did make us feel rather elevated, particularly as we actually had greenery, which was most abundant in the grounds surrounding St Peter's Church. Most other streets were devoid of foliage of any description.

We had a cinema, The Hackney Grand Central. Its entrance was in Hackney Road, and on the corner stood a stone Grecian urn-style water fountain. No water spouted from it, but if you pressed a button on the mounted brass lion's head, water would pour from the mouth. Chained to the fountain was a galvanized iron mug from which we would drink. It had a dreadful metallic taste, I hated using it, but there was no other alternative. Pressing that button to release water to cup in your hands, or drink directly from its mouth, was a physical impossibility as it had a circular stone surround, with a small channel that gathered water before it ran away, and so prevented you from drinking directly from the spout. The channel was often blocked with people's paper debris, sometimes to the point of overflowing which left you standing in puddles of water to get a drink. We had no knowledge then of sanitation. How, or why, we never caught a disease from that horrible iron mug remains a scientific mystery!

Half-way down the road was St Peter's Church, with an adjacent church school of the same name. Further along we had "our" public house, The Oxford Arms. We considered it "our pub", it was used by the family at regular intervals and whenever relatives visited us. It had large rooms above that were used for functions, particularly weddings. You always knew when a wedding party was in progress by the amount of confetti lying outside the pub on the pavement, and the music and voices coming from above the pub.

Next door was Jones the dairy; both pub and dairy were later demolished by a bomb during the Blitz. Most of the dairies around the East End at that time were Welsh-owned. I recall a dairy in Gossett Street that actually had two cows in a small barn-like structure at the side of the dairy, something I had never seen before or since in the whole of London! At the bottom, on our side of the street, the end house formed an apex. One side of the house was in St Peter's Avenue and the other side in Kite Place. It was occupied by Mr Abrahams and his daughters; Mr Abrahams, bespectacled with a walrus moustache, was a cobbler whose front room-cum-workshop on the ground floor faced Pollards Row and Gossett Street. Whenever you passed Mr Abrahams' window, he would be there, boot nails in his mouth, working away at a boot on a last, always giving you a nod as you passed by. Near to Mr Abrahams was Mr Irons, the confectioners and newsagents. They had a cigarette machine at the side of the entrance door; it was a Kensitas machine which, for 2d would dispense a very slim packet of two cigarettes with a Swan Vesta match alongside each one. Kensitas cigarettes were unmistakable by their logo of a butler dressed in black tails holding out a tray. Mr Irons, a very obese grey-haired man, and his lame wife would stand behind their counters, the shop's shelves festooned with jars of sweets. His counters sagged under the weight of newspapers, magazines and comics: *The Daily Sketch*, *News Chronicle*, *Titbit's*, *Everybody's*, *Picture Post*, *Lilliput*, and many other papers and periodicals now long gone.

As a young boy, to walk into Mr Irons' shop was like walking into Aladdin's Cave. The colours of the confectionery in glass jars on the rows of shelves would bedazzle and excite the taste buds. To watch Mr Irons carefully weigh the sweets on his scales and empty them into a small white paper bag became a performance, though what you could buy with a halfpenny or a penny was very limited. I entered a raffle in their shop one day and completely forgot about it, returning for something or another a few days later, when Mr Irons informed me that I had won first prize. It was a model of the Queen Mary. How elated and happy I was to win such a wonderful thing, to go home and proudly display such a beautiful prize! It made my spirits soar. I often wonder what became of it.

Through the course of the week, from the early morning milk deliveries by the milkmen from the United or Express Dairies, with the chinking of milk bottles and a yodel, our street had its callers all day long, with rag and bone men and with pot and saucepan repairers. New saucepans were hardly ever purchased; the pot repairer plugged the holes, or you could buy a pot-menders' kit and repair them yourself. Then there was the knife and scissor sharpener, who honed your knives and scissors, sparks flying everywhere from the grindstone wheel he was pedaling away on; often there was the glazier, panes of glass strapped to his weary back, bent from his weighty load, his cry of "Windows to mend" ringing out. We also had an occasional visit from the chimney sweep, a black-smudged face with his bundle of brushes carried over his shoulder. In the evenings you would hear the cries of "dog winner" from the vendor selling the sheet of dog results from the London dog tracks. Some of the rag-and-bone men would come by horse and cart, a round-a-bout on the back of the cart painted in the patriotic colors of red, white and blue in Union Jack fashion. You handed him your old clothes, but if you had none, you would have to pay him a penny for a ride. If you had clothes to give him, you were given the ride and a goldfish in a glass bulbous bowl. On one visit from the rag and bone man, I benevolently gave away my father's best grey flannel trousers for a goldfish and a ride on the roundabout! My mother, having found out what I had done, went running around the streets to locate the rag and bone man to retrieve them. I gave her further anxiety by putting the goldfish to bed, laying that poor creature on top of some rice pudding in her bed for its supper!

On Sundays the street really came alive. In the mornings we had the Church Lads Brigade, marching through playing drums and bugle, occasionally followed later on by the Boy Scouts and Girl Guides from the Red Church (St James the Less). Later in the morning, we would have the Salvation Army station themselves outside our house forming a circle, singing hymns to the playing of concertinas and tambourines, a few prayers and a sermon or two thrown in for good measure, and a vendor selling winkles, whelks, shrimps and cockles. Winkles were always a favourite for an East End Sunday tea, accompanied by sticks of celery. Today, I can't even look at a winkle, but then hunger was always on the agenda and you ate literally anything that was put before you. Then there was the Muffin Man, who sold his muffins and crumpets, ringing his bell. A barrel organ would later appear, its music giving the street a very happy atmosphere. It is a great pity they are no longer heard around the streets. The Walls ice cream man would ride his tricycle through, the slogan was "Stop me and buy one". The ices were made from frosted water ice inside a triangular carton, and as you demolished the ice, you would push it to the top of the carton, usually finishing up with a handful of colored water! Later in the afternoon a couple of fellows would come along, roll out a tap board and start to tap dance and sing. It was much later in life that I understood they were gay, known in the East End as "Irons", Cockney slang for iron hoofs — poofs. We would all sit on the curbside and watch them perform. I loved it when Sundays arrived; it was one huge round of lively street entertainment, merriment and activity.

There were many families down the street who were extremely poor. They stood out, as they carried an air of poverty, their faces telling everything. Devoid of merriment, their body language gave the signs of futility, and their faces had a look of despair. It never entered my head to realise that we were also poor; we simply never gave it a thought. Fortunately we were not as badly off as many others, you just didn't know anything else; there was nothing to compare it with.

Sunday also meant regular visits to the market. The Flower Market in Columbia Road, just two streets away, would begin its day with the sleepy street coming to life. The whole morning would be spent moving in a continual throng from the Flower Market through to Petticoat Lane via Brick Lane. There is something about a market that has forever held its fascination; its atmosphere, colour, and its characters, the yelling, shouting, haggling and the banter from the vendors.

The many tongues becoming a symphony, the crowds a moving canvas.

We would look at the flowers, plants, trees and shrubs, and listen to the shouts and cries from the sellers as we struggled through the crowds. If you were canny you would visit the market when it was close to closing down as prices would become rock bottom rather than the traders having to hold on to their stock. In Columbia Road there was a Gothic structure that always appeared incongruous compared to the rest of the area. I, like many others, must have passed it a million times without questioning why it was there, or how it came to be there.

Columbia Road Flower Market began in the nineteenth century, not as a flower market but a market of assorted stalls selling all kinds of different produce, spread along the full length of Columbia Road. In 1864 the benevolent Baroness Angela Burdett Coutts had the inspiration to build a market square within Columbia Road, to provide cheap food and fish from the then thriving East Coast ports. The plans included a large Gothic-style building with shops surrounding it, and flats above to provide affordable accommodation for the traders. After the church-like structure known as Columbia Market was erected, the enterprise failed and the traders returned to the street.

Leaving the Flower Market we would walk on through to the "Shallorams", a strange name used only in our family. The name had baffled me for years, as indeed it bewildered the rest of the family, but it was a Yiddish word for something old and worn. "Shallorams" was something we thought my grandmother had made up. It was a street of second-hand clothing, practically the whole of the East End shopped there. You would find people tossing over bundles of shirts, some with evidence of soiling on the shirt tails that you attempted to ignore and pretend wasn't there! Vendors without stalls would have their garments in the curbside on a bed sheet or canvas. Here you would see people trying on hats, coats, and furs. Piles of clothing churned over, money exchanging hands, and prices being haggled.

Walking through to Club Row where the cats and dogs were sold, you could find every breed under the sun, sometimes even a monkey or two. Then, on to the Bird Market with the chirps and cheeps and whistles and an array of colours of the plumage of our feathered friends, all ready to be sold. Canaries, budgerigars, finches, parrots and a hundred other varieties of birds in small boxed cages hanging on the street walls.

Brick Lane would have its greengrocers' stalls and seafood stalls, the bagel lady, the jellied eel stall serving white porcelain bowls of jellied eels with hunks of white bread. The eels were embedded in a heap of transparent jelly, sprinkled with vinegar and peppered, with five or six pieces of eel to the bowl. The flesh was removed from the bones in the mouth, and the bones spat out onto the pavement and into the road. Indian seamen would come from the docks, mingling through the throngs of people and buy sewing machines to take back to their ships, and finally to India.

Then there was Cheshire Street; with the drink stall showing the wonderful liquid vibrant colours of pineapple, strawberry, raspberry and orange and sarsaparilla, which in summer were served cold and icy and would have the mouth watering! In winter, hot blackcurrant was the number one drink, not forgetting the roasted chestnuts and baked potatoes.

The mobile van could always be found, cooking apple fritters heavily coated with sugar, and other stalls selling second-hand false teeth and spectacles, second-hand shoes and just about every commodity in existence, both old and new, that one could imagine.

The Jewish delicatessens did a good trade outside in the street with their barrels of pickled herring, and inside, chopped liver, chopped herring, schmultz herring, smoked salmon, Vienna's (sausages), hot latkas and rye bread were readily available.

We used to sing a song that immediately brought Petticoat Lane and Brick Lane to mind:

I went down the Lane to buy a penny whistle,
A copper came along and took my penny whistle,
I asked him for it back, he said he hadn't got it,
Aye, aye, copper knob you've got it in your pocket!

Everyone dressed up in their Sunday best, men, women, and children alike. Men took the trouble to wear a collar and tie, a bowler hat, or a derby. A few donned an Anthony Eden (hat) and in summer these hats would be replaced with a boater or a panama.

Men would place a pocket watch in their vest pocket, an Albert strung across either side of the waistcoat, giving an air of stature and authority. They just loved to stick their thumbs into the lower arms of their waistcoats when being addressed, displaying that watch chain, with the stomach pushed out to its full extent. Why — it was almost like being the Mayor of Bethnal Green! Invariably as you walked down the street there was a piano playing in the front rooms. Several households possessed a piano, each house you passed playing a different tune, and the music emanating would merge into one melodious casserole. The smell of the Sunday roast cooking stimulated the appetite and aroused the taste buds. The front room windows facing out on to the street had their lace curtains parted to display a plant of some description; the aspidistra seemed the most popular, on a polished wooden stand or an upright gramophone cabinet.

Now and then as you passed a window, a curtain would slowly be pulled back. A face could just be seen, the best part concealed behind the curtain, interested only to see who was passing.

Quite a few of the families had dogs of well-known breeds; we were situated quite close to the Dog Market just off Bethnal Green Road. Airedales, Chows, Fox Terriers, Red Setters and Cocker Spaniels seemed to be the favourites, with a mixture of mongrels. It was quite commonplace, if the dog was black, to call him Nigger. It wasn't considered derogatory to use that word then, it was an accepted name without any racial overtones — it would not have entered anyone's head to question it. I shudder to think of how people would react if they were to use that name today, bearing in mind that in those days a black person was a rarity.

One of the few coloured people we ever observed was an Indian who would come down the street once a year selling "Indian Toffee". He tinkled a little bell to draw your attention, made a small cone from newspaper and placed the Indian Toffee inside the cone; it was a tinier version of candy floss. The other one was known throughout Britain as "Prince Monolulu". He was a racing tipster who you would find in Petticoat Lane practically every Sunday, and was always very easy to spot in a crowd. He was quite tall, wore brightly coloured clothes, and a head dress of highly coloured plumes. His favourite slogan was "I gotta horse". A prince he was not. His real name was Peter Carl MacKay. He claimed he was a Chief of the Falasha Tribe of Abyssinia. But he was born in St Croix, now part of the US Virgin Islands. He was regularly featured in a radio programme at the time called *In Town Tonight*.

Racial discrimination then, with the exception of some of the Jewish population, was never an issue. The anti-Jewish feeling was mainly stirred up by Sir Oswald Moseley and his Blackshirts, who preached their anti-Semitic doctrine around the East End. Little did I know that several years later when my curiosity took over, I would find myself drinking in his company!

Pubs were invariably full on Saturdays and Sundays; they were the poor man's opium, the working man's only form of temporary release from the drudgery of work, and away from the responsibilities of wife and kids for a brief period in their humdrum lives. To get drunk was a way of life; it wasn't anything unusual to see a drunk at the weekends. The pubs had a saloon bar, a public bar and a small off-licence bar for outside orders. Beer was served "loose" for people bringing their own jugs.

The public bar was a man's domain, quite spartan, sawdust thrown on the floor, perhaps a dartboard, but you rarely saw women there. The saloon bar was better furnished with reasonably comfortable tables and chairs and always a piano. Most women would accompany their husbands on a Saturday night to the pub's saloon bar; it was the one occasion when they could get themselves "dolled up". Invariably a pianist was hired for the weekend, popular songs were played and usually a sing-song entailed. At the weekend you would see children outside the pubs waiting for their parents. They were usually given an Arrowroot biscuit to keep them quiet; this was a very large sweet biscuit that pubs sold in huge glass jars at a penny a time.

An accordionist would visit the pubs around the locality; he would stand outside and play a popular medley of songs, then go into the bars with a hat for a collection. Quite near to us in Old Bethnal Green Road was Lou. He was known to all of us; I can see him now, trilby hat, thin pencil moustache, cigarette dangling out of the corner of his mouth, a club foot that made him limp quite badly, the heavy accordion strapped to his back on his way to the next pub. The Salvation Army would come into the pubs on a Saturday evening selling their War Cry; hardly anyone would refuse them. Many of the pubs would have clubs, members paying in every week to provide a good dinner and Christmas presents come the highlight of the year. It was not unknown for a Christmas club's treasurer to suddenly disappear shortly before the festivities, leaving the poor subscribers "high and dry"!

One day, bandy little Ginger Jago, the youngest of the very poor Jago family from Nelson Gardens, took a jug to the Oxford Arms to be filled up with beer. Albert Poole, the publican, went to fill up the jug and found a bed bug at the bottom of the jug. Remarking to the young boy that there was a bug in the bottom, young Ginger quickly responded, "That's nuffink, we've got fahsands of 'em at 'ome"!

The whole Jago family was bandy. Mr Jago was a bookies' runner; you would see him standing on the corner of Nelson Gardens and St Peter's Avenue outside the Oxford Arms, on the lookout for the police and for the punters who would come along and place paper betting slips into his hands — the transaction being made as discreetly as possible. Should a policeman be spotted, Mr Jago would beat a hasty retreat down Nelson Gardens to his home at the very bottom of the cul-de-sac, out of sight.

On some Saturday nights Grandfather might be in a benevolent mood and take my grandmother out to a public house, usually the Oxford Arms. It was the only time she had occasion to dress up, which was usually all in black. She would overuse the powder puff and wear every piece of jewellery that she possessed. We dubbed her "Nancy Glitters"!

If ever you entered a pub around midday during the week you would find a few women sitting at a table sipping a glass of ale, wearing flat caps like the men, shelling peas for dinner, the pods of the shelled peas falling into their aprons that were collected up after the apron was full. It was a great place for a "jaw", the term they used for a good chat.

Nelson Gardens formed a "U" shape from St Peter's Avenue and back again. We had several school friends living there who also attended St Peter's School. Among them were the brothers George and Teddy Evans. Teddy talked me into joining the church choir and Johnny Renshaw, who when Sinatra became popular went completely overboard, and never stopped imitating him!

A girl who I liked very much was Iris Renfrew. I gave her my signet ring and Mother went berserk when she heard that I had given it away and promptly went round to the girl's mother and reclaimed it. It was a romance that finished before it began, and although she was an attractive girl at the time, dear Iris became quite plain and lanky later in life, married and went to live in Norah Square. The strange thing was that having grown up together, whenever we passed each other in our adult life, words of recognition were never exchanged!

On Monday mornings it was commonplace to see a queue forming outside Walter's the Pawnbrokers in Hackney Road. His full name was Leonard Moules, and Grandmother always referred to him as Walter Leonard, but we knew him as Walter. I can see him now standing behind the counter with his twirled waxed moustache taking in the bundles of clothing and other items from the queue that regularly formed there at the beginning of every week. Grandmother would say to us, "go in the front door, not at the side door in the alley". It was considered that only the real hard-up cases went in the side door. The "old man's" suit or watch and chain went in regularly on Monday morning, coming out by Friday in time for him to go out at the weekend.

But tragedy was to come for Walter. On 30 April 1942 at 10.23 p.m., P.C. Clement April, in the company of other police officers, went to the premises of a pawnbrokers shop at 299 Hackney Road, having heard a dog barking in the basement, and found a door partly open. He had trouble in opening the door, and when he flashed his light he found a body behind the door. The body was identified as that of Leonard Moules (Walter), aged seventy-one years. At the Coroners' inquest, Detective Inspector George Keen was engaged in making enquiries into the death of the deceased. It was mentioned that £40 and a quantity of rings had been removed from the safe. On 9 May, two young men, Samuel Dashwood, aged twenty-two years, and George Silverosa, aged twenty-three years, were charged with the willful murder.

The evidence of a fingerprint expert had discovered somebody's palm print on the safe in the shop. Subsequently he received the palm prints of Silverosa from Brixton Prison and it was of his opinion that it was made by the left hand of Silverosa. Dashwood had been discharged from the Army the previous August as a result of his mental condition. The accused were committed for trial at the Old Bailey.

Dashwood dismissed his counsel, resenting the fact that they considered him abnormal. Their petitions for reprieve were dismissed and they were sentenced to death and executed at Pentonville Prison on 10 September 1942. Later on, the bombing devastated the area surrounding the pawnshop, but it was one of the few buildings that survived.

In our young adventurous days, we used to climb into the pawnshop where poor Walter had been murdered. It was silent, dark and eerie. We climbed the stairs to the top of the building and all we could hear was the creaking of the pulley ropes of the service lift that ran from the ground floor to the top floor. The noise of those ropes creaking began to scare us. Our thoughts were focused on the murder that had been committed in the building. We fled down those stairs "hell-bent for leather" and out of those premises, never to return!

Dying, and funerals if you could afford them, were very stately affairs and considered an event. The house of the deceased would have its front room shutters closed — several others down the street would have their blinds half-lowered as a mark of respect. The undertakers, normally English's from Bethnal Green Road, came with their horses and carriages. The horses were black and harnessed in black leather, with silver embellishments and purple feathered plumes on their heads. The carriages were also black, polished to such a high degree that you could see your reflection in them; the undertakers wore black top hats. The direct relatives were always attired entirely in black, the women wearing veils, while other mourners wore a black armband or a black fabric diamond sewn on to their sleeve. Family mourners would remain in black for at least three months. Neighbours gathered outside the house on either side until the coffin came out, and remained until the coffin was placed in the hearse and the entourage moved off. Neighbors were left to talk amongst themselves and pass their comments to say "what a lovely chap", "what a lovely person she was" or "what a lovely turnout they gave them". If ever you were walking along and a funeral procession happened to pass, it was customary to stand still, raise your hat if you were wearing one, or if you didn't, touch your coat collar, and remain still until the procession had passed as a sign of respect for the departed. I really never understood why we touched our collars. Anyone who could not afford the full services of an undertaker would call on my grandmother and ask her to lay the body out. She would wash them, comb their hair and make the corpse more presentable. If it was very hot weather, she would cut an onion and place it under the bed to hide the body odours of the corpse. She would return to our house and tell us how nice he or she looked, saying what a lovely hair parting she gave them. My sister would cringe in horror at being told about the dead. My grandmother would tell us that if you didn't fear them in life, you would most certainly not fear them in death.

Many families had children of an age group similar to my sister and I, so we grew up together, played together, went to school together and remained together until we became that much older when, through diverse circumstances, we went our separate ways. There were the Arrowsmiths, the Andrews, the Kendalls, the Baldwins, the Gardeners, the Wards, the Mills, the Radfords, the Dearings, the Herberts, the Hudsons, the Beauvoirs, the Smiths, the Heywoods, the Kilburns, and so many other names. For some unknown reason the women would address each other by their surnames. Sometimes passing by their doorways, you would find a child sitting on the doorstep eating an enormous size piece of bread with "Daddies Sauce" or granulated sugar, or perhaps jam, spread over it. If it were a Monday it was usually a piece of Yorkshire pudding left over from Sunday's dinner, dipped in condensed milk.

The Dearings were one of the wealthier families in our street, often referred to as "Big Pots". Anyone with wealth was regarded as "Big Pots". They had a nicer furnished home, the children were better dressed. They had two red Chow dogs with purple tongues, which were forever in and out of their mouths, dripping wet saliva. We firmly believed that if you were bitten by one of the Chows with their purple tongues, they would poison you. So in our ignorance we kept clear of those dogs if we could! Their youngest boy, Ernie, and his older sister, Betty, would at times invite us to play in a small building at the back of their home that stank of the dog's droppings. It had a small stage where we would hold a concert of sorts but would never have given us entry into The Royal Academy of Dramatic Art!

On Sunday mornings it was commonplace to see pony and traps out, as it was a Sunday pastime for those who could afford it. You would be walking along, and suddenly that familiar sound would get nearer and nearer, the clip, clip, clopping at a very fast pace until they were alongside you. The ponies were beautifully groomed, the driver dressed up in his Sunday best with his whip in hand, with the trap gleaming; they were a showpiece, a lot of effort went into preparing pony and trap for their Sunday morning jaunt — you just could not help but admire them!

On Sunday afternoons we made a point of being outside the Dearings' house, as Mr Dearing would arrive home by taxi. A taxi down St Peter's Avenue was a rarity, with the exception of Mr Dearing's Sunday homecomings. He would alight from the vehicle, cigar in his mouth. The smell of a cigar would be associated with wealth, and I loved that smell. If you were lucky enough to be close to him, he would give you a sixpence; we would then buy sweets and share them with the other boys. To be given a whole sixpence was, for us, to be in seventh heaven.

The Hudsons and the Beauvoirs moved into the street shortly before the outbreak of war. They occupied the larger type houses with four or five steps leading up to their entrance doors. In summertime those families would sit out on the steps watching the world go by, something the other residents would never dream of doing. They were a rough and ready lot by comparison, lacking perhaps in social graces, very blunt, calling a spade a spade. On first impressions one

26

would be put off by their appearance, yet they had hearts of gold, and once you got to know them, they would do anything for you. Despite their coarse nature, they were good people. One day, the insurance man called on Mrs Hudson to collect. It was apparent that she was in no position to pay him. Before the poor man had time to get off his bicycle she said "You can fuck off for a start"! Mrs Hudson's diplomacy was non-existent, she knew no other way to express herself! When there was no money around to feed your family properly, the rudeness and profanities acted as a defence mechanism to ward people off.

The Hudsons were extremely hard-up, with a family of eleven. Their youngest daughter Renee was doing handstands one day with some other girls; they used to do them up against a brick wall. To the dismay of the girls, they saw that poor Renee wasn't wearing any knickers! My Aunt May, on hearing about this, promptly went out and bought the girl a couple of pairs. Renee turned out to be an attractive, eloquent lady; sadly she died of cancer at the age of twenty-seven.

Approaching September, the exodus of thousands of East End families would begin, making for the Kentish hop fields. Some of the families in our street, who were no exception, would travel with their babies in arms. The hop picking season lasted three weeks. "Hopping", referred to as 'opping, meant that lorries were hired to collect their essential family possessions, piled high with their mattresses, pots and pans and all the other necessities required for the season. It was their form of a holiday, albeit a working one, to get away from the rent collector, insurance man and any other person who might make payment demands on them, to be far away from the East End, far away from the everyday struggle for survival. Many of these families would write to the same farmer every year so that they could return to familiar surroundings. The quarters they stayed in were quite ramshackle, austere and basic, but come the end of the day when work was done, they would enjoy a sing-song and booze-up, joining other families whom they had befriended during the hopping season. They would return to the East End looking rosy-cheeked and healthier from Kent's fresh air. It was not too long before the pallor of the East End returned.

If you wanted one of your playmates to come out and play, you would go to their front door, "holler" through the keyhole shouting "Door, door, coming out, coming out". If they were finishing their meal you would be asked to come in and sit in the passage until they were ready. Many times if it was raining, we would sit in the passage of one of the homes with a pack of cards, playing snap until it had stopped. I was never allowed to have boys in our home who played cards, they were considered bad luck.

There were six of us boys who were always together. I would not describe ourselves as a gang, we never thought of it as such. We were all born in the same year, went around together, left school together, and stayed together right up until our teenage years when our tastes and interests began to diversify. Horace Andrews, 'Orrie always appointed himself as the organizer, even writing and producing school plays that we participated in. When I think of the names of those boys now, I wonder what became of them; Jimmy Arrowsmith, his younger brother Peter, Ernie Gardener, Johnny Kendall, Horace Andrews and Peter Ward. I always remember young Peter Arrowsmith accompanying us to the cinema. If anything of a scary nature was shown on the screen, he would lower his head behind the seat in front of him so he couldn't see! We would have to tell him what was going on, amplifying the frightening scenes to make him even more scared. I guess we were just plain shockers!

Further up the street lived Gladys Sampson. She was a tall, gangly girl who always looked like she had just crawled out of bed, and had a Terry Thomas gap in her front teeth, while her hair was hardly ever groomed. Gladys in her younger years was "boy hungry" and when she became older, "man hungry". At school, she sent 'Orrie Andrews a three penny piece to go out with him. I never discovered whether 'Orrie returned that three penny piece, or kept it. One thing for sure, he most certainly never went out with her! Like many girls in the East End, going "Up West" at the tail-end of the war in pursuit of Yanks was an attractive venture. Gladys was no exception. At weekends, she would paint her face heavily with make up, lips thick with lipstick. She would board a bus in Hackney Road and head for the West End of London. The American GI's had far more money to spend on the girls than us. They would buy them gifts such as silk stockings that they hadn't seen for years.

29

Street games were played in a regular seasonal pattern. It often puzzled me how one game that lasted for a few weeks would suddenly be succeeded by another without anyone organising the change, they just happened to follow on, one after the other. There would be the whip and top, marbles or "glarnies" which we carried in little cloth bags, those beautiful pieces of glass coming in every colour of the rainbow, some with coloured streaks running through, and we would roll them along the gutter in the road. The larger ones, "glarnies", were used as a prize; that is, if you could hit it, it was yours. Those missing the target would be retained by the owner.

We also played yo-yo's and hoop-la. If you didn't have a wooden hoop, a bicycle wheel with the spokes removed, with just the metal rim, served as your hoop. Hop-scotch was chalked out in the road, as were tin can copper, knocking down ginger, roller skating, ball games, cricket, with the wickets chalked up on a brick wall.

When skipping we would sing:

> Rosy apple, lemonade, tart
> Tell me the name of your sweetheart.

You would then proceed through the letters of the alphabet, and if you caught the rope on a given initial, that would be the letter your sweethearts name began with.

The other skipping song was:

Salt, mustard, vinegar, pepper.

If you were bouncing a ball the song was:

> One, two, three a lairy
> My ball's gone down the airy
> Don't forget to give it to Mary
> One, two, three a lairy.

The "airy" referred to the exterior basement area of the larger houses in our street, and was an opening beneath pavement level covered over by an iron grill; adjoining the airy was the coal chute. There were heavy circular iron patterned plates set into the pavement, to be raised by the coalman when delivering his coal by horse and cart. He wore a leather type hat, the back of which reached almost halfway down his spine, to protect him from the coal dust.

Aunt May, who lived at No. 2, had her coal delivered by the coalman who lifted the iron plate directly into the basement area. Our coal would be carried through the house and the sacks emptied into the coal cupboard under the stairs. Each time the coalman from Lebon's of Dalston would visit, he would receive a "coating" (telling off) from our grandmother She was always complaining about the size of the pieces of coal, and that she was only getting sacks of coal dust. On most occasions the lumps of coal were too large to be placed on the fire — you would invariably have to smash them with the poker to fit into the fire grate. I think those poor coalmen dreaded delivering to our house!

Boys or their fathers made scooters, the front board having coloured-metal bottle caps attached, displaying your lucky number or the number of your house; some scooters would even have side carts. We would scooter to Victoria Park and the Hackney Marshes, a considerable distance from Bethnal Green, stopping off sometimes at my nan's home in Clapton. She would give my friends and I tea in the garden. I loved her poppy seed crusty bread, the butter spread on the bread like a ploughed field in miniature, made by the marks from the blade of her serrated bread knife. Hand carts were made from an old pram chassis. We would make our own swings from the plaited straw rope that bananas were tied in, and discarded by greengrocer stallholders in Bethnal Green Road. The rope was tied to both sides of the crossbar of a street lamp, forming a loop that you could sit on or whirl yourself around by using your feet. Our favourite lamppost was outside Mrs Smith's house on the corner of Nelson Gardens. She would come out and tell us to "sling your bleeding hook" — her polite way of telling us to go! I guess we must have been a source of annoyance in our over exuberance at play. We would stand at the top of Hackney Road by the tram stop asking the alighting passenger for their cigarette cards. At the time, every cigarette manufacturer would have a series of picture cards inserted in the packets. Some of these cards were quite beautiful, ranging from warships, military regiments, famous film stars, and flowers etc; little did we know that many years later they would become quite valuable. We would stick the cards into albums or use them in the school playground to flick down a card held upright, usually a rarer one that you did not have from a set you might be collecting. We would also collect the silver paper from any empty cigarette packet, wrap the paper around our index finger and form the silver foil into the shape of an egg cup. We would wet the base of the cup with our spittle and throw them up to the ceiling; sometimes they stuck, other times they did not! It did however give us a sense of achievement to see your little silver cup on the ceiling!

We would also collect bus tickets, and each denomination would be of a different colour. Bus conductors wore a peaked cap and uniform, a leather bag at their side for change, a small handheld wooden rack that would hold the bus tickets which ranged from white, blue, red, pink and green. The conductors would come down the aisle of the bus shouting "Fares please!". Many were natural born comedians and put people in a cheerful mood on their way to work, with others a little more serious. Bus inspectors hopped on and off the busses regularly checking for anyone trying to dodge a fare.

On some Sundays we boys would take a return journey by tram to the Kingsway Subway in Holborn. The shake, the rattle and the roll of those trams, especially if you happened to be sitting at the top, added to our delight; the highlight of the day was entering the subway in semi-darkness. To us, it was a thrilling day out.

Those of us who had roller skates would skate down Blythe Street, known to us as "Jews Alley", as practically all the residents there were Jewish, using the houses not only for living in, but also for garment manufacturing. We liked skating there as the street had a smooth asphalt surface that made it a pleasure. On many an occasion some of the Jewish residents would ask us to light their fires, or turn their lights off on a Friday evening, their Sabbath or "Shobbas" as it was known to them.

Our purchased weapons were either a catapult or a peashooter. The catapults were used on targets like tin cans or old deserted factory windows. Peashooters were used among ourselves, our missiles were brown lentils bought from Gunn's the Chandlers and Corn Merchants in Bethnal Green Road. We never did wanton damage or vandalized anyone's property. Law and order was held in high esteem, our misdemeanours and antics were minimal, and we also had a great respect for our elders, and never thought otherwise.

Crime in our street was non-existent. Some people would have their house key tied onto string that made it accessible by putting your hand through the letter box, pulling the string to reach for the key to let yourself in. Burglary of houses was unknown. There was nothing in the homes worth taking!

Muggings and rapes were also unheard of. The East End, to walk around at night, was secure, and never at any time did you feel threatened or unsafe. The East End villains would target Mayfair, St John's Wood, Kensington, all the wealthier boroughs to carry out their burglaries. If they happened to get caught, they accepted it with good grace saying, "Fair cop guvnor."

The only thing criminals really feared was "the cat" (cat-o'-nine-tails) and the younger ones "the birch". Sentences and punishments were so much harsher then.

In the colder months we would play games in each other's homes. Black man's dark scenery was a game where we hid under a pile of coats and had to guess who was beneath it. There were doctors and nurses, mothers and fathers, when we would explore each other's anatomy, usually the nether regions which held more interest than other parts of the body! The girls were just as inquisitive as the boys. It was a natural innocent curiosity which made a boy want to see what the girl's private parts looked like and the girls wanted to see what the boy's willy looked like. The very word "sex", or any thought of such, was never heard or thought of. We never even knew where babies came from!

We used to play our cricket and tin can copper in Nelson Gardens alongside St Peter's Church, the bottom half being a cul-de-sac. We called this area Le Bealing; funny name, we never knew where it came from, but I suspect that it was the name of a previous cabinet maker at one time. The existing cabinet maker's factory would have the smell of menthylated spirits and polishes that hit you if the factory doors happened to be open. In the morning and afternoon breaks, a tea boy would emerge, usually an apprentice, with several tea cans hooked up on a broomstick by their wire handles, dirtied and stained with polish from the constant handling to get filled up from Harry Orsi's

Café in Bempton Street facing the church. He would return later with the steam rising from the cans of piping hot tea, the broomstick perched firmly on his shoulder, a package of cheese and ham rolls wrapped under his arm. In the afternoons the package would be cakes. Cabinet makers, French polishers and upholsterers were the main forms of industry around Bethnal Green.

Adjoining the cabinet makers was an area sectioned off by a brick wall with broken glass at the top to prevent anyone climbing over. We really believed that a witch lived behind that wall! Occasionally, when we were playing, we would hear an old woman's voice shouting at us to "clear off", and we ran to escape her in fear of her casting of a spell on us.

This same area was reserved for Bonfire Night. There was a large circular inspection plate in the middle of the road which I think must have been an entrance to a sewer. It served as a base for our bonfires. We made our "Guys" from any old clothing stuffed out with newspaper, a papier mâché mask placed across the head with an old hat perched on top. The Guy would be put in a pram and wheeled around the streets, asking for a penny for the Guy. Later in the day the Guy would be placed in Hackney Road by the tram stop, so that we could stop returning workers alighting from the trams and persuade them to part with a penny! The pennies we collected would buy our fireworks. The guy would always be placed on top of the bonfire for burning.

There was a fellow we all called Tucker, and we never knew where he lived, only that he was related to a couple of families in the street. Tucker was always dressed in a black suit, with a black flat cap we called a "cheese cutter" tilted to one side of his ginger head, his complexion was always as white as a sheet, while his lips had a slight tinge of blue; I suspect he must have had a rheumatic heart and that he was somewhat retarded. Tucker would nominate himself to be in charge of the bonfire; he seemed to be able to acquire more wood than anyone else for the fire. One bonfire night Tucker came with a box full of Beecham's Pills, I think he must have pinched them and he handed them out to all of us kids. We thought they were sweets and swallowed several of those little pills. Lo and behold, we were in and out of the toilet a few hours later, and some never quite made it in time! Tucker was out of favour with our mothers for many months. I, in my innocence, did something very similar not long afterwards when I bought a packet of exlax thinking it was chocolate, and gave our little team of boys each a piece before we went off to the cinema. It was not too long after the performance began that there was a mad dash to the toilet — almost in unison! There was another character around the same time as Tucker known as Nugget; we didn't know his real name. His mouth was permanently open which exposed the only tooth he had in his head, heavily stained from smoking. It resembled a fang if anything, and like Tucker he was a little retarded. His appearance was off-putting and a little frightening to some of us, although he meant well and was always trying to be friendly and give us things, things that we believed he had removed from an unsuspecting proprietor of the local shops. We were just too young to understand that he was simply just trying to be kind and that he was lonely.

Bonfires were piled quite high with old furniture and anything inflammable that we could lay our hands on. We would place potatoes onto the fire until they were blackened and charred, retrieving them with a stick. We would dance around the fire like Red Indians with flaming pieces of wood. On one occasion my ear got burnt quite badly — my grandmother took me to school the following morning and remonstrated with one of the teachers. What on earth this had to do with the school, I could never quite fathom, but that was my grandmother!

Comics were regularly exchanged, from the *Film Fun* to the *Dandy* and *Beano*. There were cartoon characters like "Desperate Dan" with a gargantuan appetite, usually finishing up with a "cow pie" with horns sticking out of the pastry. Dear Keyhole Kate was always peeking into keyholes, never minding her own business. The *Film Fun* had comic strips with Laurel and Hardy. I used to imitate Laurel crying at the kitchen door. Arthur Askey and other stars of the day would also be depicted in cartoon form. As we became older, the more juvenile comics were discarded and we would read *The Hotspur, The Wizard* or *The Champion* with short stories of Sexton Blake, Tailspin Tommie and many others of characters long forgotten. Stories of rockets to the moon and outer space were beyond our comprehension, and to believe that by 1969 a landing on the moon would become a reality was unimaginable!

The cinema was a great escape from the poverty around us. To see Fred Astaire and Ginger Rogers, Busby Berkeley's kaleidoscopic dance routines, the sophistication, the glamour, the debonair men in white tie and tails, Nelson Eddy and Jeanette McDonald in *Rose Marie, New Moon, Rosalie, Girl of the Golden West* and many other films took you a million miles away from the East End as you sat there transfixed by the silver screen. We loved Eddie Cantor in *Roman Scandals*, the Marx Brothers, Shirley Temple, Our Gang, Freddie Bartholomew and a little boy singer called Bobby Breen who sang "There's a rainbow on the river". On one occasion I befriended a boy in Dalston who showed me how to bunk in. I accompanied him feeling very nervous by what I had done as we found seats and sat there on needles and pins throughout the whole performance of *The Firefly* with Allan Jones and Jeanette McDonald. Allan Jones sang "Donkey Serenade". How I loved his voice and that song!

We had several cinemas around us that we frequented. The Odeon and the Grand Central in Hackney Road, the Standard in Goldsmiths Row, the Excelsior in Mansford Street and Smarts in Bethnal Green Road, which used to have wooden benches until it changed its name and became the Rex, The Foresters and the Museum in Cambridge Heath Road, The Regal, the Empress and Hackney Pavilion in Mare

Street. It was not uncommon to have a film break down, and if ever this happened the audience would whistle, yell and shout at the projection box; the longer it took to repair the film, the louder the noise became, until the film resumed playing. Cinema attendants were dressed either in maroon, blue or green livery with gold aiguillettes worn from the shoulder and peaked caps with the name of the cinema embroidered with a descript motif on the front of the cap. They would line up the patrons in queues according to the price you were paying. A chromium stand would display "Standing Room only in the one and nines" (1/9d). They would yell "Full up in the nine pennies (9d), no more seats", carrying their torches like a Field Marshal's baton. There were times when one of us would get a bash over the head from a torch for "bunking" into the cinema. At the Grand Central there was an iron bar missing from the gent's small toilet window that we were able to crawl through. The other method we used was to get wire from the orange crates from the greengrocer stalls in Bethnal Green Road; a hook was made with the wire and passed through the fire screen doors; the hook registered onto the crash bars, pulled the bar down and released the door. What an ingenious lot we were when money was hard to come by!

The Odeon Cinema in Hackney Road was the last cinema to be built in our locality; it was the most luxurious cinema around, with the plumpest upholstered seats ever with padded arms, so beautiful and comfortable to sit on, and thick carpeted aisles that felt like walking on air! It was our very first taste of anything luxurious. The other cinemas by comparison were "bug 'oles". The earliest films I recall seeing there were *The Count of Monte Cristo* with Robert Donat and *The Adventures of Marco Polo* starring Gary Cooper. The Odeon became my favourite; it was a little bit of heaven just to sit there. The Regal was next in line for a better class cinema. At intermissions an illuminated electric organ would rise up from the ground before the screen, colours flashing from the organ and changing as the music was being played. At times songs were displayed on the screen and the audience would join in singing.

Outside the Grand Central in St Peter's Avenue, a vendor was based at the curbside selling Percy Dalton's Famous Roasted Peanuts from a wheelbarrow. If you went in the cinema on the second or third performance, you walked almost knee-deep in peanut shells, empty ice cream tubs, cigarette packets, with sweet and chocolate wrappings around your feet, the air thick with cigarette smoke, so thick that an attendant would come around with a spray gun and spray over the audience a cheap perfumed vapour.

The performances then were greater value for money, giving far better entertainment than today for an evening out. You had the "A" Feature film, the "B" Feature film, a comedy "short" of either Three Stooges, Charlie Chase, Andy Clyde or other comedy "shorts". The Movietone News or Gaumont News came next — the narrators of the newsreels with their clipped, cut-glass accents, and then the trailers of forthcoming attractions. The actors and actresses were shown before the commencement of the film, giving the names of the roles that they were playing; even the secondary players equally known to us were displayed in this fashion. Quite apart from the stars, you knew every supporting player in the film. Zazu Pitts, Nancy Kelly, Guy Kibbee, Eric Blore, Edward Everett Horton, Hugh Herbert, James Gleason, Frank McHugh, the names went on and on, great character actors. At the end of every performance the national anthem was played, and people would rise up from their seats and stand to attention for the duration.

Our grandmother would sometimes take us to an afternoon performance, either to the Hackney Central, the Excelsior or the Rex. The Rex was formerly known as Smart's, where one would sit down on wooden benches. She would take a shopping bag that contained an alarm clock, a bottle of cocoa and some biscuits. The alarm clock would be set in case she dropped off to sleep. This occurred on several occasions when we were sitting with her. The rest of the audience never appreciated the clock's alarm bells sounding off in the middle of a film!

On Saturdays, having made some pocket money, we would go to the Standard in Goldsmith Row. We called it the "Two Penny Rush", pronounced *tuppeny rush*. The Standard was very much "a bug 'ole" as well, although as youngsters, we didn't really care. The seats were wafer thin, upholstered in rexine (imitation leather) with brass studs, so if you sat long enough your behind began to ache, shifting the cheeks one side to the other. To enter the auditorium was like bedlam; between 200 and 300 kids yelling and shouting at each other before the performance commenced! Our favourites were the serials of Flash Gordon battling against Emperor Ming, *The Adventures of Rin Tin Tin* the wonder dog, and of course, the cowboy films. Cowboys, like Tom Mix, Ken Maynard, Tim Tyler, Buck Jones, and Hopalong Cassidy. Comedies would also be shown like the Three Stooges, Andy Clyde, and Wheeler & Wolseley. We would vacate the cinema feeling like cowboys, pretending we had horses, holding out our arms as though we were holding reins and instead of walking, we would trot, making horse noises! At other times we would emulate some of the antics of the Three Stooges. Whoever had an impact on us at the time, we would invariably copy. Opposite the Standard was a fishmonger, selling wet fish and ready-cooked cold fish. If we had a penny or two to spare, we would buy a piece of cold fried fish and devour it in minutes.

Watching those cowboy films did have some influence on us; we regularly played cowboys and Indians. We had toy cap guns that were quite heavy, made from a cast metal. In those films you would often see a cowboy hitting another over the head with the butt of the gun. One day, I re-enacted this scene on a boy I was playing with, landing the butt of my gun on his head which immediately streamed with blood. He ran home. His elder brother came out and chased me through the streets, but never caught me and fortunately for me the matter did die down. That boy,

Eddy Woollard, became an Amateur Heavyweight Boxing Champion.

The postmen in those days wore a hat more like a helmet, somewhat Germanic in style. Our regular postman had a large carbuncle on the back of his neck which made you feel as though you wanted to stick a pin in it, and make it disappear. Postal deliveries were prompt and efficient, and occasionally a telegram boy would appear down the street on his bicycle, wearing a pill-box hat held by a chin strap, a belt strapped diagonally across his upper torso holding a shiny patent rectangular pouch where the telegrams were kept. An official armband was worn on his sleeve displaying the Royal Mail crown. Usually they would be cycling to their next telegram delivery, whistling away, full of the joys of spring.

In the evenings the lamplighter would appear on a bicycle, his long pole perched over his shoulder. He would hook up the metal arm of the lamppost, gently raising it until the gas mantle was at full glow. Come daylight, he would repeat his rounds to turn the gas lights almost off. The cat's meat man would also deliver by bicycle, a large basket affixed to the front beneath the handlebars, piled high with sliced horsemeat, newspaper wrapped, and if you were not at home, he would leave the cat's meat under your knocker, or wedged in your letter box. Our cat's meat man was the brother of my grandfather's best friend. He had rather a vacuous looking face, gold-rimmed glasses with tiny lenses, and an "old bill" moustache. My aunts dubbed him Clark Gable and he was known as this by all the family, never as the cat's meat man.

Running behind horses and carts was a favourite pastime, the preference of these being Charrington's the brewers' dray horses and carts, towing a cart loaded with beer barrels at a very slow pace. We used to perch ourselves underneath the cart on the ladders, used for rolling the barrels down into the cellars of a pub. These ladders were secured by chains, and the motion of swinging side to side and the plodding of the horses made it a lovely illicit little ride.

In the summer time we would watch Carlo Gatti's, the ice makers at the foot of the canal bridge in Queensbridge Road, sending huge blocks of ice cascading down the chutes from the factory onto the carts. Carlo Gatti's horse and cart drivers were big, dark-skinned, muscular Italian men, mostly wearing a Garibaldi moustache, who tossed the ice blocks around with their huge ice tongs as if they were cubes of sugar. They hoisted them up on to their shoulders protected only by sacking to prevent water from the ice dripping on to them, and stacked the blocks until the carts were fully laden. Carlo Gatti's carts were unmistakable, painted in bright canary yellow and black. We loved to hitch a ride in the summer time and purloin some of the ice that had broken away from the large ice blocks that were being delivered to cafés and restaurants. If we managed to filch a piece, we would suck on it until it was small enough to place in the mouth.

Occasionally, if you were seen clambering on to the back of their cart trying to remove some ice, the driver would think nothing of raising his whip and lashing out at you. If you were seen running behind a horse and cart, someone always seemed to be there to shout out "Look behind you guvnor" — never pronounced governor. Fortunately throughout my days of running after horse and carts, I never received a whip lash or any other form of injury! Motorization had not reached its peak, and the horse and cart was still very much in vogue.

The horses' droppings left lying in the road were never there for long before a bucket and shovel would emerge from one of the houses, whereupon it was scooped up for garden manure. My grandfather made a point of being alert whenever a horse appeared on the street to be ready to shovel up the horse's poop; if you heard a clip clop, you would be out of the house immediately! Some people would go around the streets gathering up the horse manure and selling it.

Our grandfather's garden was his pride and joy. Many others down the street preferred keeping chickens outside instead of a garden to provide them with fresh eggs, and from time to time a chicken dinner; the poor chicken would be dispatched when her laying days were over. Some even kept rabbits for the same purpose, not only as pets but as a source of food. Mrs Baldwin next door kept chickens; she had no garden but managed to grow a few large sunflowers looking over the wall into our garden. To me those flowers always looked hideous; they were ugly and really not attractive at all. The rest of her space was just a dismal area of black soil where her chickens would be clucking away and pecking into it. Mrs Baldwin always looked very stern. She was a large woman always dressed in black, her hair plastered back into a bun with a centre parting, a woman of very Germanic appearance who found great difficulty in raising a smile — in fact I cannot ever recall seeing her smile at all. Grandmother and Mrs Baldwin were never exactly neighbourly.

Mrs Hudson kept her chickens in the "airey" (small outdoor space adjoining the house at basement level), a most unusual place to keep chickens! In the hot weather Mrs Hudson could be seen through her iron grating, chickens running around her, fag in her mouth, feet in a bowl of water, peeling potatoes and placing the potatoes in another bowl beside her.

Summers seemed hotter then. We boys would sit by the roadside well away from the drains where pink disinfectant powder had been placed by dustmen who came along in their horse and carts. It was believed that if we played near the drains you would catch scarlet fever. We dug up the melting tar from the tar blocks that made up the road, a weird pastime that fascinated us! Sitting there plunging a matchstick into the tar and lifting it from its blocks, removing it and shaping the tar into little balls. My mother had just bought me a pair of white flannel trousers — I could not think of a better time to wear them. I came home with my trousers covered in tar and she went absolutely ballistic! As a summer drink, Grandmother would give us R. White's Cream Soda with milk; I guess it must have been a poor man's milkshake, although in those days we had never heard of them. If we were lucky we would have a vanilla ice cream placed in a glass of cream soda. This, to us, was a summer drink above all other summer drinks. Ginger beer came in two-tone stone bottles; these were used as hot water bottles in the winter.

There was a small road linking St Peter's Avenue to Warner Place named Bempton Street. It had a café there whose proprietor was Harry Orsi; we pronounced it "'Arry Orseye". Harry was Italian and had once been a chef at one of London's leading hotels. His café had been a motor repair shop that was converted into an eating establishment. He was overweight and limped quite badly. He had a permanent ulcerated leg problem, the leg swathed in bandages, which at times worked loose and trailed around his feet, of which he seemed completely unaware. I suspect that he must have been diabetic, but in those days people didn't know about such maladies. At the weekends he would make the most fantastic ice cream ever and sell it from the front room window of his home in Nelson Gardens.

His café, like many others in London, had a large chromium tea urn on the main counter, and the lower counter displayed large plates of cakes, cheese rolls, ham rolls, Doubleday's meat pies and many other edibles on show to tempt the palate. He served a hot meal at lunchtime which attracted many lorry drivers who could park unseen from the main road. One particular cake he served was what we at that time called a "cheesecake", although it never had the taste of or resembled a cheesecake in the slightest; a round pastry tartlet with a plain sweet filling, icing over the top with shredded coconut embedded into the icing. That man also cooked the best egg and chips in London! It was to be the bane of my mother's life, since I often ordered his egg and chips, telling dear Harry that my mother would pay — she did, of course, always settle up with him; she seldom scolded me for my audacity. I do reiterate even to this day they were, without question, the best egg and chips I ever tasted! His chips were thick cut and unsurpassed in flavour! A bottle of Tizer (red-coloured fizzy drink) to accompany the meal was, to me, like nectar of the gods.

As a source of earning a copper or two, we would run errands for some of the neighbours; we would canvas by knocking at doors crying, "Any errands, any errands?" Invariably it would be a "no" but sometimes you would strike lucky and have an errand to run. This gave us money to buy sweets from Belsham's on the corner of Warner Place and Bempton Street. Old Mr Belsham reminded me of the "Old Bill" character from the First World War. He had a greying walrus moustache, was rather corpulent, and always wore a heavy black cardigan and a flat cap that he never removed! Depending on how much money we earned, we would buy a sherbet dip: yellow lemonade crystals that we sometimes watered down to make lemonade, but mostly we wet our fingers and dipped them straight in to the crystals to suck on. There were acid or pear drops, bull's eyes, jelly babies, liquorices sticks we called "Spanish" and every other confection that might take your fancy. He would blow into a small white paper bag to make an opening to pour the sweets into from his weighing scoop. If we could not afford the sweets we would buy loose mustard pickle, served up from a large stone jar, and placed in newspaper or desiccated coconut.

In Old Bethnal Green Road in a small terraced house we knew as "Silks" we would buy homemade toffee apples. Their front room window was used as a shop window, and apart from toffee apples and bundles of firewood, I don't think they sold anything else; it was just another source of income.

Warner Place was situated just west of St Peter's Avenue; it had two public houses, the Baker's Arms and another called "Moaners", which we never knew by its true name. It was given its name by a one-time publican that was always moaning, and the name stuck! Towards Hackney Road there was a cabinet maker by the name of Spiers. One of his children, Morris, was a playmate of ours. Morris had jet-black wavy hair, a cast in his right eye, and the most unusual laugh; it would have pauses in between the bursts of laughter. His laughter was the oddest I had ever encountered, very low in tone and almost sung! We would play in the yard at the back of his father's small factory on piles of wood shavings, but unfortunately there was dog's doo-doo amongst the wood shavings which coated my hands on more than one occasion, so I decided not to play there with him anymore.

On an errand one day for a neighbour for a loaf of bread, I went to Wasm's the Bakers in Hackney Road. Arriving at the main thoroughfare, the road was cordoned off; trams were not running, and traffic was at a complete standstill. A very large horse stood in the middle of the main road, with blood pouring from its numerous wounds. The poor thing had bolted and gone straight through the shopfront window of the bakers I was about to visit. I stood there looking at that sorrowful animal; the scene upset me and remained with me for several days. Inquisitive crowds had gathered, watching that poor beast bleed to death. Eventually a couple of men came and led him away into Ion Square and shot him. When the entire furore was over and things were back to normal, I went into the bakers for the loaf; blood was still on the front window display which assistants were scrubbing in an attempt to remove it. From behind the counter an assistant weighed the crusty bloomer loaf, and also gave me a square piece of mince. Normally this would have been devoured before I arrived at the recipient's address, but on this particular occasion it was the only time that I had lost my appetite.

At other times to earn money we would scout for wood suitable for firewood. When we had gathered up enough, we would chop it into convenient sized sticks, bundle it up, tie it with string and sell it. We never had any problem selling firewood, transporting it around the streets in an old pram shouting "firewood". The local shops couldn't compete with us, we were that much cheaper.

CHAPTER
TWO

Our Parents

They met at Miss Youen's Dance Classes at No. 18 St Thomas's Square in Hackney. Everyone knew it as Mother Youen's, and you got three dance lessons for 2s 6d. Father played clarinet and violin there and helped out with the dancing lessons, as he was very good on the dance floor. It was an age of sophistication and refinement. Father, I believe, modelled himself on a smartly dressed screen actor by the name of Adolphe Menjou, who wore a different suit in practically every scene he played. His work over the years was mainly in hotels, with an occasional stint as a temporary librarian. He was extremely knowledgeable of all the good restaurants and hotels in the West End of London, taking a great interest in food and was indeed, like my mother, a wonderful cook and a great lover of classical music.

Our parents were married on 6 December 1927 at the Registry Office in Hackney; they resided at the time at No. 33 Balls Pond Road, Hackney. Mother was named Elizabeth Georgina and Father just plain Henry. The family called my mother "Niddy" — how she came by that name I will never know. Families seem to give nicknames to their offspring only familiar to themselves. Three children were to follow; Henri was born in 1928, and he died eighteen months later of meningitis. Sister Dawn entered the world in 1929 and I followed the following year.

Looking back on our mother and father's relationship, it was not too difficult to understand that they were really not meant for each other. It was hardly a match made in heaven, though it is easy to see how they were attracted to each other. Mother, in her younger days, was a very striking woman, the most attractive of all her siblings. Father was tall, slim, sophisticated, well-read and well-spoken; they married when father was twenty-two and Mother was twenty-one. Regretfully, neither of them was cut out for parenthood, nor for that matter, wanted the responsibility of having children. They were poles apart both in their outlook and interests and came from two different worlds.

At some stage during Mother's first pregnancy, they moved into our grandparents' home in St Peter's Street. With Father living in such a cramped and unfriendly environment, he found that conditions, and the relationship with his in-laws, were too much for him to bear and he could take it no longer. One day he just upped and left. It was about this time he met a girl with whom he fell in love, and continued to love throughout his life, and even though she eventually married someone else she remained in his thoughts, and he carried a photograph of her in his wallet until the day he died.

When my mother heard about his relationship she gave him a verbal onslaught that lasted years; she sought him out at practically every place he worked, not caring in the slightest how she embarrassed him. She loved him, so could not take the rejection kindly. It was to last a lifetime. On the day he left No. 74, a very vivid day in my memory, she ran after him all the way up the street calling him names. I ran behind them crying my eyes out. It was one of the saddest days in my young life.

Growing up without our father left a great abyss in our lives. Children can be quite cruel and very often we were taunted for having no "ole man". For a man to leave the home was considered something alien to the East Ender. It took a long time to reconcile ourselves that our father was no longer with us. We no longer had his love, his affection, or his guidance.

Mother worked in the West End and the City as a waitress. Sometimes she would come home very late from a wedding or a banquet, bringing with her some of the left over tit-bits from the various functions she attended. This was considered an enormous treat; to have fancy food that we had never seen or tasted before. It was readily and easily devoured. She gradually acquired additional pieces for the home which included a gramophone. We didn't have much of a selection of records at that time; consequently you would play the same record over and over. My earliest recollections were playing a song called "Steamboat Bill", and the whistle of the steamboat would sound off several times during the course of the song — I just loved to hear it. Another was "It looks like rain in Cherry Blossom Lane". We had another record that used to be played that would depress both my sister and I called "On we go through the snow". It depicted prisoners being marched through the snow, eating carrots as they went singing "On we go through the snow" (we only knew it as a song of this title). It was as though a black cloud had passed over you and left you in a state of despair. Even to this day, if ever we refer to that song, it has the same effect upon my sister and me as when we were children. Mother could play the ukulele and Father often played violin in a professional band. Mother could strum out a tune and sing "Dinner for one please, James". Sometimes if he had the money, he would bring us home delicacies such as Jewish Vienna's (sausages), Halva and stem ginger in lovely oriental stone jars.

Father had a peculiar sense of humor. One winter, my sister and I were quite hungry. He raised our small box-room window, collected some snow, and made some snowballs gathered from the window ledge, placed them in a frying pan, and lit the gas stove.

My sister and I stood by in total silence and watched the snowballs turn to water! He thought it was funny, but on reflection I think he was trying to humour us and take our minds off the hunger — there could not have been any money in the house for food.

He befriended a Jewish family, the Silvers, who lived at The Oval leading off Hackney Road. The Silvers were from Russia. Old Mr Silver, who spoke little English, would play Russian and Jewish folk songs on his concertina whenever we visited. We would be offered cake and lemon tea, and sometimes they would entertain us by hanging up a white bed sheet and perform behind it by candlelight, creating silhouettes, although I was too young to understand what they were supposed to be playing. They would have an intermission and drinks. The whole family were quite mad and their antics reminded me of the Marx Brothers. Tony Silver remained a friend of Father's for several years until he became mentally ill and was committed to an asylum. Father visited him once or twice; poor Tony did not recognize his friend and thought my father was Raymond Navarro, a silent screen film star! One of Tony's other brothers took up the piano at the age of fifty-eight years, and became an accomplished player of classical music.

When Father was living with us, he would take us to see our paternal grandparents. We called our grandmother Nanna Sue. They, with our three spinster aunts, lived in Clapton. Clapton was then a lovely district; it was considered quite posh by Bethnal Green standards. I loved going there! They lived in Ashenden Road, where each house had a bay window and a walled or iron railed front garden. In summer, residents would leave their front doors wide open to allow cool fresh air to enter, covered only by a canvas door awning. When he took my sister and I, it was never by tram or bus, we walked the whole way. Whether or not he could afford the fare we never knew, but walk we did. Their house was a pleasure to visit, with the smell of lavender and furniture polish everywhere, a far cry from our home in Bethnal Green. They would allow me upstairs to play in a room that housed all their stock reserved for selling on their stall in Chatsworth Road. I always made a beeline for a large box that contained buckles and buttons in various colours, shapes and sizes that kept me amused for hours on end.

Mother was a complex character. She would make an effort to appear sophisticated and put on the "accent" if she thought it was required. Strangely enough, all of her sisters — with the exception of Marie — did the same thing! Her accent could change from a gentle "Gor blimey" to Mayfair at the drop of a hat! She took great pains with her appearance and was always smartly dressed whenever she went out. One great asset to her character was that she was a hard worker. This was a family trait, and no one in our grandparents' household was allowed to be idle.

One Sunday morning, shopping in Brick Lane, she met a neighbour and they started chatting. During the course of the conversation, the subject of bad language was brought up. Mother was telling the neighbour how much she detested its use just as a dog leapt up at her. She immediately shouted "Get down you bastard!". Nothing could more aptly summarise or be more descriptive of our mother than that incident!

Our paternal grandparents were kind, gentle, conservative people and our three spinster aunts, Lil, Joan and Enid were very well-read. All the family were great readers and even at our young age, they would introduce us to books to read, as indeed our father did. Enid, the youngest, was the fun one — a little

57

bohemian, extremely artistic, a great mimic, and she made the most beautiful dolls.

It was interesting to hear that later on our aunts embarked on a family search and discovered that we were Huguenots — long before genealogy became popular. My great-grandfather was a naturalist and before him they were all gentlemen, going back to 1645. Our father was to end his days at the Huguenots Apartments and French Hospital in Rochester, Kent.

Huguenots can be traced from 1689 when they settled in the East End of London around Spital Square. They made an enormous contribution to the economy from their expertise as silk weavers, watchmakers, silversmiths and financiers. By 1700 there were nine French churches in the East End. The first was built in Threadneedle Street and the other at the Savoy. One of the churches in Brick Lane became a synagogue when the Jewish people lived in the area; it has now become a mosque. The very fine architecture of the houses built by the Huguenots still stand in and around Spitalfields. They arouse a great deal of interest amongst visitors to the area.

One day Nan took us to Chalkwell on the Essex coast. It was the very first time we had ever seen the sea or the seaside. Having never seen it before, we were both captivated and enthralled; it was like being transported to a magic land! The sun was shining, the skies were blue and we saw a beautiful expanse of sea! Nan bought us buckets and spades, we built sandcastles, paddled in the sea and chewed and sucked on a stick of rock. We ate sandwiches she had brought from home, while she sat back in a deckchair reading, occasionally dropping the book into her lap and looking out to sea. She was so quiet and reserved, unlike our maternal grandmother in Bethnal Green. That day was so wonderful, we never wanted it to end, and we never wanted to return home.

We called our paternal grandfather "Little Harry"; our father was "Big Harry". Little Harry had a hosiery stall in Chatsworth Road which my father sometimes looked after. Next to the Castle Cinema in Chatsworth Road was a café — well, it was really what we termed "Dining Rooms"; each table was sectioned off by a wooden partition. When Father wasn't working the stall, he would have his break there, playing dominoes with some of his associates. He won at dominoes so many times his friends dubbed him "Harry the fox". He would buy me a college pudding and custard. I loved those puddings! It was always something to look forward to when going to visit him in Chatsworth Road.

In 1938, Mother opened a café in the Haggerston area, in a small lock-up shop in Scriven Street that ran from Queensbridge Road into Haggerston Road. I must have been her most frequent visitor! She was an excellent cook and it was not long before she established a regular clientele. I would help out either washing up or sometimes running errands when I was not at school. She had a helper from time to time, an elderly lady we called Emma, who was able to tell fortunes from tea leaves left in a tea cup. One rainy afternoon when the café was quite full, I was sitting with Emma and my mother asked her to tell my fortune. Gazing into the tea cup I had drained, she proceeded to tell me that I would see more countries than anyone sitting there. In time, Mother decided to move to much larger premises in Haggerston Road. It had accommodation above the shop with much better facilities.

Ashamedly, one day I removed a two shilling piece from her till, and placed it in the cigarette machine for a packet of "Craven A" cigarettes. Together with my play friends we went down an alley and smoked some of them. I became quite giddy, began to vomit and felt dreadful! I knew that I had been punished for removing that two shilling piece!

By this time, she had extended her working hours by opening up on Sundays, selling seafood outside the premises. The seafood came up by train, fresh from Leigh-on-Sea to Fenchurch Street Station. Mother may have been lacking in many things, but she was never work-shy.

By then, I was spending more time in Haggerston than in Bethnal Green. One day, I ventured into Ridley Road Market in Dalston. Ridley Road then was predominantly a Jewish Market. Jack Solomons, the fight promoter, had a fishmongers there. Barrels of pickled herring were at practically every shop and stall you passed. The Boobas and Yentas (grandmothers and talkative women) there would be haggling over the price of fish and kosher chickens, giving the chickens an inspection more thoroughly than guardsmen on parade would ever hope to receive! Yiddish was spoken more than our own tongue. This was Ridley Road. It was not uncommon for some of the local boys to pinch florins and half crowns from the open wooden tills on the stalls; one immediately recognized what a boy was up to when you saw him racing through the crowds, away from a stallholder that he had just taken money from.

In the market I once saw a huge crowd of people dressed in black shirts, with armbands bearing two streaks of lightning, which I later learnt was the party emblem. Shortly there was a huge roar from the crowd and arms were raised in a "Seig Heil" Nazi-style salute. It was then that I saw Sir Oswald Moseley. He was standing high in an open car, returning the hordes' salute. His followers were going wild at seeing him, the frenzy and adulation gradually dying down when the car came to a halt and he prepared to speak. The whole scene was as daunting as it was awesome. I stood watching this man, not really understanding what he had to say, but carried away by the whole spectacle. I was not around that long to see if any fights and scuffles took place. It was well-known that these meetings, which were so well publicized by the newspapers, sparked off battles between the Blackshirts, and the Communist Party and Jewish organisations. On Saturday evenings after all the stalls had been cleared away, we would go to Kingsland Road to "The Waste" and sort over the debris from the stalls. When I think of what was thrown away, I realise now it would have made an antique buyer very happy! If one could only have had the foresight then.

Prior to the outbreak of war, Father took us to Lyons Corner House, Coventry Street, in the West End of London. To go "Up West" was always an exciting adventure. Lyons, or Joe Lyons as they were known, had a string of tea shops throughout London, which were easily recognizable by their white painted shop fronts and gold lettering. Their standards for quality, cleanliness, and affordability were about the best you could get.

We entered the restaurant, found a table, sat down and Father proceeded to order a selection of pastries and tea. They were brought to us by one of the waitresses who were known then as "nippies". They all wore the Lyons uniform of black dress, short white apron and white cap. The waitress placed the tea on the table and the pastries were nicely arranged on a two tier cake stand. Father began to talk to us in earnest, saying, "You see those pastries, take a good hard look at them before you eat them, because you are not going to see anything like these for a long, long time." Talking to us so seriously had a profound effect on us. It turned out that he was absolutely correct; we did not see them again until a long time after the war was over. We never forgot his words.

Father came to see us occasionally and gave us treats, taking us to the cinema in Dalston Lane, buying a box of Black Magic chocolates to devour in the course of the performance — he was a chocoholic! We saw Gracie Fields in *Shipyard Sally* — that wonderful soprano voice, as she sang "Wish me luck as you wave me goodbye". "Our Gracie" was loved by the nation, as indeed was another artist at that time, George Formby.

Father would also take us to wonderful places of culture, such as the British Museum, the Science Museum, and the Natural History Museum. Pointing out and explaining things, he gave us a history of the exhibits that we revelled in. And he introduced us to books, arousing our interests in those he recommended that we read. These visits were to cement my lifelong interest in history and the arts.

Unlike our grandparents in Bethnal Green, our other grandparents in Clapton had an Anderson Shelter installed in their very long garden. Father had taken me to visit them. While he was in the house, I was left outside playing in the garden. I found a pot of bright blue paint and a brush and decided to paint the front of the shelter; on completion I thought it looked quite nice. When Father and Little Harry came into the garden, Little Harry normally a quiet and reserved man, went absolutely ballistic. An argument ensued between Father and son over my "artwork". I couldn't quite make out what all the fuss was about. I really thought that I had done a splendid job. Little Harry obviously thought otherwise!

CHAPTER
THREE

Life at No. 74
St Peter's Avenue

Our address was No. 74 St Peter's Avenue — the house I grew up in. The very mention of the number catapults me back to Bethnal Green, whenever I see or hear it.

At the time of my childhood it housed fourteen of us! Grandfather, Grandmother, my mother and father, my sister and I, our uncles Will and Joe, plus their friend Alf Schofield, our aunts May, Lilly, Marie, Eileen and Winnie, and another aunt, called Ethel, whom the family called Noona. How she came by that name was never known to us. Noona left No. 74 when she married a man named George Marshall and went to live in Walthamstow. Marriage for many became a form of escape. It was claimed that our grandmother had fourteen children in all: two sets of twins and two others who died. Fatalities in childbirth in her day were very high. There would have been five in our immediate family but for the loss of our brother Henri (he died eighteen months before I came into the world).

Records state that I was born in the Bethnal Green Infirmary, 214a Cambridge Heath Road. I never liked the sound of the word "infirmary"; it has connotations of poverty and debtors prisons. The Bethnal Green Guardians purchased the Cambridge Heath Road site in order to erect a new infirmary. The site had previously been Bishop Hall Farm but was leased in 1811 by William Sotheby to "The London Society for promoting Christianity amongst the Jews". It became known as "Palestine Place" and schools and houses followed.

The site was purchased by the Guardians in 1895 and the new infirmary built to accommodate 670 patients. The total cost of the land and buildings was £212,895. Many of its furnishings were made by inmates of the Waterloo Road Workhouse in Well Street, Hackney. The Hospital was opened 5 March 1900, and included a Nurses' Training School within the administration block. During the wars, the Infirmary was utilised as a military hospital. The hospital closed in 1990, and its staff and patients transferred to the new Bancroft Unit at the Royal London Hospital.

At home all our aunts, with the exception of Aunt Marie, married and gradually departed to live elsewhere with their spouses. Marie joined the Salvation Army in a permanent capacity and moved to various places around the south of England, eventually becoming a Brigadier. On the day my grandfather learned that she had enrolled in "The Sally Ann", he went absolutely spare. I had never seen him so enraged. He was brought up a Catholic, and although we never knew him to attend church, he was very rigid in his beliefs. He regarded the Salvation Army as a lot of "Bible punchers".

An uneducated man, but as honest as the day was long, his favourite quote was, "Tell the truth and shame the Devil." His parents had hailed from County Cork during the Potato Famine in Ireland. He possessed a jaundiced mind on matters he never really understood. A Labour Party man through and through, he could never explain why he was a socialist, he just fell in line with the majority. If ever you mentioned conservatism, his feelings and that of many like him were "what have I got to conserve?". The general consensus was that the Tory Party was restricted solely to the wealthy. His views on homosexuality were just as bad. In his day, a homosexual was referred to as a "nancy boy". "Put 'em up against a wall and shoot the bleeding lot of 'em" was his philosophy. Homophobia was then an unknown word; he was an East End product of his era.

He once told me that my maternal great-grandfather was a master japanner and grainer who, before the First World War, would specialize in painting public houses. All the masonry and stonework would be japanned and grained to look like wood, either a light oak grain or a mahogany grain, whichever the publican preferred. Work like this would take him approximately three months to complete; it would be painstaking, fine and intricate work. He would be paid in gold sovereigns, then proceed to go on a binge for several weeks, alienating himself from his family! He would go to Smithfield Market to buy a whole belly of pork, bring it home and roast it on a spit over a fire in the basement of the beautiful Georgian house in which they lived, smothering the belly of pork in mustard without removing his bowler hat and eating it alone, away from the family. At the end of his boozy period he would return to work to commence painting another public house.

My earliest recollection at No. 74 was of being in one small back room sleeping on the floor with my mother, father and sister. A small gas stove stood in the corner and a small food cupboard sat opposite. The picture becomes a little blurred as to how long we actually lived like that, but when my uncles married off and Alf Schofield married our Aunt May, we finally had a bedroom with our very own beds. Looking back, I still feel a sense of amazement how we ever managed, but manage we did. There was no water facility upstairs. It was carried up both to drink and wash with in an enamelled bowl. Lighting was by gas. Around the wooden disc that gave rigidity to the gas pipe holding the mantle, we would see bed bugs crawling about; small reddish brownish insects about a quarter of an inch long, with oval flattened bodies. They were resilient little buggers that we would squash with our thumbs and once squashed they gave off a sweet odour that I can almost smell to this day. We never knew a household without bugs. The pesticide appliance used then was a hand-compression gun that contained a small round tank of "Flit". Flit was a brand name disinfectant that was sprayed on to the affected areas. Trying to eradicate the bugs was a thankless task as they could spread from building to building, room to room, hiding in every crevice; they were the Romanies of the insect world which had little to do with the level of cleanliness.

The hall on the ground floor was never called a hall, it was always referred to as the passage. On either side of the passage before you reached the front room door, hung two pictures framed in light walnut depicting battle scenes from "The Charge of the Light Brigade". I would look at these pictures for lengthy periods. They were so animated and coluorful, and the uniforms, the swords, lances and sabres would intrigue me. Further down the passage was a horse stand of bamboo and cane, and a mirror in the centre with a cane box beneath it. On the lid of the cane box stood a red china elephant. It had a castle-like structure on its back that would have been used for a tiger shoot had it been life size. That elephant became so embedded in my brain, I found that I started sketching it at every given opportunity. I drew it at school, painted it at school; in fact I became quite adept at drawing and painting elephants. This was a start of a lifelong love affair with drawing, painting and art.

District Nurses were a common sight in the East End, cycling along in their unmistakable navy blue uniforms and navy blue hats. Somehow or other, I contracted worms. The District Nurse called to attend to my malady, coming up the stairs to the bedroom with her bag of medicinal tricks. She pulled out of her bag an enema tube and a bag. She showed me what looked like wood chippings, which I think were Quasha chips. She placed them into a receptacle of boiling water and left them to take effect. Satisfied that the mixture was right, she then proceeded to siphon the liquid up into the rubber enema tube and proceeded to pump it up into my backside. I could feel the warm liquid swishing away inside me. Sitting me rapidly over a bed pan she removed the enema tube, and the liquid gushed out, along with hundreds of little worms wriggling about! It must have been an early method of colonic irrigation. She came for one or two more visits, after which I was free of worms. The District Nurse provided an invaluable service to the East End.

While Mother went out to work, we were left in the care of our grandmother. Gran as we called her was about the hardest working woman I have ever known. She was no taller than five foot, if that. She had a job in the Strand at Shell-Mex, charring (cleaning the office). She would set off around six o'clock each weekday morning, and some days bring home brown bread rolls and cigarette ends, the largest cigarette ends she could find. Most of the brown rolls were for the widow Mrs Andrew opposite, as she had been left with four children to bring up. There was Teddy, Alfie, Hetty and Horace. Alfie permanently suffered from a red soreness around his eyes, grandfather always referred to him as the boy with the "salt beef eyes". They were so poor that they couldn't even afford a gas mantle; the bare flame would be the only form of lighting. I used to take the cigarette ends to "Old Moore", as my grandmother called him, who lived in Pollards Row, a continuation of our street. He would sit on the steps of his house, break the cigarette ends open, mix up the tobacco and roll them into cigarettes. To all intents and purpose he should have died years before, but he lived well into his nineties. Inhaling all that smoke and bacteria from those dog ends over the years, he defied medical science!

Home from her "charring" in The Strand, Gran would commence box-making for a company in Hackney Road, The Stanley Box Company. Glue, and the smell of glue on the gas stove, was forever under our nostrils from morning to night. My sister and I would assist her in box-making, cutting the corners out of the cardboard which would cause blisters between our thumbs and index fingers. She would then glue the glossy coloured paper to the boxes. She hated making pen boxes that were small and fiddly. On completion of two gross or more, the boxes were tied up, and we would place them in a pushcart and take them to the box company to be paid. Payment was paltry, something like a penny farthing for a dozen boxes. Prior to our being paid, the boxes were checked and we were then given a new batch to take home. If what they had given you were awkward or fiddly to assemble, Gran would bemoan you as if you were personally responsible! When she was cooking, you would have the combined smells of glue and food. She also ran a loan club for Phillip's and Scoons in Bethnal Green Road. She washed all the towels used by the teachers at our school. She never had a holiday in her life, apart from days out at Southend, which were very seldom. If she managed a trip there she would be on "needles and pins" to get back home. In the winter I would see her out in the yard doing the washing, scrubbing away on a washboard submerged in a galvanized bath, her arms red raw from the detergent. The larger clothing items would go to the bag wash. To come home from school and see laundry drying on the fireguard in front of the fire with steam rising up from the wet clothing would set me into a depressed mood. I hated Mondays, and the bad mood it placed me in never lifted until all the washing was put away.

Our grandmother was an atrocious cook. Perhaps it was the size of her family that never allowed her the time to undertake any really good cooking, or perhaps she was just not interested. I think it was the latter. Sunday lunch, we never called it lunch, it was always dinner, was about her best effort. Normally it would be a joint of beef, pork, lamb or salt beef. Her roasted potatoes were virtually fat free, more like a baked potato, always accompanied by a dish of sliced beetroot and one of freshly grated horseradish, marinated in vinegar. The portions of meat were very sparse. Come Monday, you would have the leftover food from the day before, and if the meat could not stretch to reasonable portions, she would supplement your meal with a chipolata or a sausage. Your meal would be covered by a saucepan lid, chop covers were unheard of, and when you raised it you would find your chipolata embedded in a pile of potato. Fortunately, we always had a bottle of Daddie's Sauce on the table, and the flavour of the sauce was better tasting than the meal itself. At times I used to let my mind take over and really think that I was eating something quite delicious; mind over matter can be a wonderful thing. There would be a stew that the whole family would enhance with Daddie's Sauce, pouring it into the pudding basins and disguising the taste. When you came home the basins would be in the gas oven keeping warm. There must have been nine or ten meals with a crust forming on top of those stews! She would ask you to take one from the oven, and as you commenced eating, you would be told that you had taken the wrong one. I could never understand why, they were all the same size basins!

The remainder of the week it was pies and mash, fish and chips, sausages and mash, or liver and bacon. Gran would make a thick liver sauce from the flour that she coated the liver in for frying and stews. Sometimes we were given soused mackerel that I absolutely loathed and dreaded whenever it was placed on the table. Fridays would be fish and chip days, never cooked at home, and always bought from Little Annie's in Gossett Street. Annie was so short her head hardly came above the marbled top counter that held jars of wallies (pickled cucumbers), pickled onions and pickled red cabbage! Fish was about a penny or 2d then, and would nearly always be skate, rock salmon or cod. When we were not getting fish and chips for the family, we would buy a halfpenny worth of cracklings, the batter that dropped off the coated fish. We would put plenty of vinegar on the cracklings and suck the vinegar that passed through the small nuggets of batter at the bottom of the cone-shaped greaseproof paper and newspaper.

I was never given any fish in those days, it would be fried egg, sausage or a couple of rashers of bacon with the fish shop chips. All the perishable food was kept in a cabinet outside in the yard, known to us as a safe. A cabinet with a narrow wooden frame, a lower drawer, and metal mesh panels on three sides of the cabinet, the top covered in an off cut of linoleum to keep it waterproof. The only refrigerators we ever saw were at the cinema. Sometimes in summer, the bacon could be a little high, sausages sour, which we would term as being "on the bugle", and the cheese a trifle pongy. If there was butter it was always a little rank. Everything was eaten regardless, we were a hungry lot! During the weekdays we never knew breakfast as such, usually a slice of bread was about all you got with a thin layer of margarine we called "marge". Butter was an almost unknown commodity, if we had butter which was very rare, it was known in our home as "best butter". Looking back I often wonder how we survived and how we never developed any sinister disease from the condition of the food we ate.

Birthdays and birthday parties were never celebrated, in fact, it never crossed our minds. We never saw a birthday cake, nor received a birthday card or present. We just never knew that a birthday was celebrated. Invitations to birthday parties by other boys and girls in the street were non-existent, like ourselves; they never knew they took place either. It was a case of what you never had, you never missed. Our cousin Sheila complained to her mother, Aunt May, that she never had a birthday cake, and Aunt May promptly made her

73

a marmalade tart and stuck lighted matches around the edges of the pastry, that is if you could call it pastry.

On Saturday mornings we would get a piece of cheddar cheese that had been on a shelf in the safe too long and hardened, and melt it in the coal-fire oven in the kitchen, creating the poor man's fondue. At times if my grandfather had not eaten his supper, such as a sheep's head, it was passed over for me to eat the following morning for Saturday's breakfast. I would pick away at the meat on its head, even eating the sheep's eye, the teeth still in its jaws! I look back now and the whole episode revolts me. In those days we ate just about anything put before us. On Sunday we might be lucky and have a boiled chicken or duck egg. Our tea would be winkles, sometimes shrimps, with bread and butter, and sticks of celery. In winter we would have crumpets toasted in front of the fire as an added bonus. I was usually given the toasting fork and would sit in front of the fire and do the toasting. When we had winkles our Aunt Lilly would remove the little caps protecting them in their shells with a pin, sticking them on her face as though she had measles!

She was about the most humorous of the aunts, a tom boy if ever there was one! I remember walking alongside her as she slowly peddled her cycle through Warner Place, when a youth passed us, uttering an unpleasant comment to her. Without any hesitation she got off her bicycle and promptly smacked him about the face! He was as astounded as I was, not bothering to defend himself, and he walked away saying absolutely nothing. She got back on her bicycle and continued cycling up Warner Place!

Aunt Lilly's pen-friend boyfriend came home from India, pulling out his "topi" helmet from his kitbag and dropping it on my head. The thought of being with someone who had just come from India excited me. I wanted to hear about the country, its people and his experiences there in the army. We never really got around to hearing much. He was from Liverpool, drank too much and sang Irish songs that delighted my grandfather, who thought that he was the cat's whiskers. He and Aunt Lilly married and moved to his native Liverpool. He turned out to be an absolute swine and a wife beater; they divorced after having two children. For reasons unknown she moved to Scotland and married a Polish ex-army officer and had a further three children.

I remember one Sunday afternoon in the winter time, my grandmother gave me a saucer of tinned salmon for my tea. It had been standing on the window ledge in the yard. Placing the salmon before me I noted that it was frozen in ice. I was so hungry that as each piece thawed out I ate the iced, watery salmon devoid of any flavor, smothering it with vinegar and pepper to enhance the taste. On another occasion Winnie, the more refined member of the family, came home; it must have been a Friday. Gran served her up egg and bacon with two dumplings left over from the previous day's stew. Poor Winnie just did not appreciate our Gran's *haute cuisine*. We had a "waste not want not"

75

policy in our household. Our grandmother was decidedly not *Cordon Bleu* material.

Sometimes we would arrive home to see Gran sitting cross-legged looking glum, her feet tapping away with the rapidity of a machine gun. We immediately knew that something had occurred that had set her off in this ugly mood. Usually it was one or two of the family who had emptied their meal in the dustbin. We then got the full blast of her displeasure, with her saying "Fine bleeding crew I've got. Go and have a look at my dirt pail." We never did of course. We ate our meal no matter how awful it was in order not to offend her any further. She had one or two sayings that for years I could never interpret. If anything was very dark she would say it was as "black as Noogits Knocker"; eventually I discovered that it referred to the knocker on the door of Newgate Prison. This had probably come from the debtors prison and using Cockney jargon, it had become distorted over the years. The second saying she used if she was amazed at something was, "Gor blimey, blind ole kill cooper". To this day, I have not quite worked out what this meant, the nearest interpretation I can find is "We'll" or "I'll" "kill or blind a cooper", a cooper being a barrel-maker. Whenever she made these odd remarks I regret that I never asked her what they meant. If any family member should come down in the morning in a none too polite or grumpy mood her quote was, "They've woke up with their arse in their hands this morning." On occasions she would ask me to go to Ellis's, the cooked meat shop in Bethnal Green Road, getting the usual purchase of brawn and luncheon meat. If my grandfather was in earshot she would say in a louder voice, "and a quarter of pound of pressed beef for your grandfather" — then whisper to me, "make it two ounces." If Grandfather happened to be at home and there was a knock on the door from a neighbour, Grandmother would answer and stand in the doorway having a lengthy chat. This used to make my grandfather irate; he would yell down the hall in a very guttural growling voice, "Come in 'ere out of it, nothing but cackle, cackle bleeding cackle." Grandmother of course would completely ignore the growling which made him even more irate. Such was a peaceful day at No. 74!

Gran's tea making was about the worst tea one could ever taste; you stood about as much chance of having a freshly made cup of tea as winning a lottery! It was simply indescribable, stewed beyond any resemblance of tea. She would leave the teapot over the gas ring to keep it hot and leave it there for hours. By the time it was poured into a cup, the colour of the tea was grey, mixed with a couple of ounces of tea leaves that accompanied the liquid for good measure! I can never recall a tea strainer ever being used.

Grandmother would take me shopping with her to Bethnal Green Road, which was a place of hustle and bustle from Mondays to Saturdays, stretching from just beyond Vallance Road almost to the Salmon and Ball. A long ribbon of canvas topped the stalls and the stallholders yelled and shouted to attract your attention. Greengrocers, grocers, fishmongers, confectioners, the cat's meat man, tinkers, drapers and hosiers all had stalls. The stalls all faced looking into the shops. Halfway through the shopping we would stop off and she would take me into Kelly's, the pie and mash shop. Kelly's also had another shop just further up the road, but we favoured the Kelly's opposite the Rex Cinema. Kelly's interior was similar to practically every other pie and mash shop in the East End, with white tiled walls, marble-topped tables, condiments of salt, pepper and vinegar, and sawdust on the floor. Trays of pies would come out from the kitchen, with a huge vat of green parsley liquid that we called liquor. It never resembled parsley sauce in any shape or form; it was more floury and less creamy, more like parsley, flour and water. A huge bowl of coarse mashed potato would be placed behind the counter. If they were very busy and some of the tables had not been cleared you would have to sit with your food amongst other people's plates and liquor spillages which formed into little puddles on the table tops. Even as a child, I hated this. My grandmother used to order herself a bowl of stewed eels, and a bowl of mashed potato and liquor for me.

Pie and mash in those days cost about 2d, a bowl of mash and liquor was half a penny. Vinegar and pepper were applied and it was eaten with relish, though I thought that Gran might have been a little more generous and ordered me a pie. She would say to me, "Don't tell anyone when we get home."

A traditional London working class food, pie and mash shops have been in London since the eighteenth century. A pie from a pie and mash shop is quite different from any other pie; it has a flaky-like pastry top, completely devoid of butter or fats, a mince beef filling with the base having the texture and consistency of a steamed pudding. They would be served with liquor and mash, always flavoured with chilli in the vinegar, and salt and pepper. In my adult life I did take one or two people along to the East End to savor our delicacy, but not being raised on "our soul food" they found it not quite to their taste! The customers nowadays in these establishments are very mixed in terms of social class, which is far removed from the "working class only" customer image. Sadly a lot of these shops are disappearing now from the East End, a great shame for I feel that this is part of our heritage.

Opposite Webster's fish & chip shop there was a stall which would be used for weighing and cutting up wet fish, or taking live eels from a tray and chopping them up into edible sized pieces. If ever I saw them doing this in winter when it was really cold, seeing their hands almost blue with cold, I would feel even colder, and it would make me long for warmth and comfort. The adjacent stall on the corner of Mape Street was the cat's meat man, with "Clark Gable" slicing away at huge slabs of horse meat and wrapping half pounds of the smelly stuff in newspaper.

I had a favourite stall in Bethnal Green Road, it was close to the Marquis of Cornwallis pub, and was a confectioner's stall making boiled sweets before your very eyes. I used to stand watching this man making sweets, absolutely mesmerized by the dexterity of his work. He would roll the confectionery into one long sausage and place it around two hooks about three feet away from each other, and commence twisting and turning at an incredible speed, finally snipping the confection into mouth sized portions. The pineapple twist, the bull's eyes, cough drops, pear drops and the sweet smells as he was making them would make the mouth water. In the dark winter afternoons and evenings, the stallholders would have their gas lamps ablaze, the lamps giving off a hissing sound. To see a long row of stalls lit up at night gave it a fairyland atmosphere. When it was really cold most of the stallholders would have a brazier burning to keep their hands and bodies warm; standing on a wooden pallet or wooden boards for hours and hours behind a stall was a feat of endurance. You would see them stamping their feet and quickly moving their arms around their shoulders to keep the circulation going. The cries from these people and their bantering, shouting out "Ripe bananas!" or suchlike, usually followed by a witty remark or rhyme, made the whole market a wonderful place to be.

At the end of the stallholder's day, everything was packed up and moved away and there remained the debris of orange crates, cardboard, paper, discarded bad and bruised fruit, and vegetables stretching far down the road. Before the council came around to clear this away, children would be sorting through the rubbish, salvaging any fruit or vegetables worth retrieving for the table. Damaged fruit would be referred to as "spunky"! With a spunky apple or orange, you cut away the bruised or damaged part of the fruit to make it edible.

On the corner of Mape Street stood Hailes, a German butchers. There were several German butchers around the East End at the time. He sold just about the best saveloys, pease pudding and faggots you ever tasted. His succulent saveloys were plump and juicy, his faggots were herby and meaty, served with wonderful gravy, and his pease pudding had a soft, creamy texture. This man had a large heated copper container outside his shop, and people would queue on Saturday nights, bringing their jugs with them to be filled with his faggots and gravy. Pease pudding and saveloys were wrapped in paper. To this day, I have never tasted anything that resembles his wonderful food. Whether it be Selfridges or Harrods, they could never have competed with that butcher's produce! We would go to Stoltz the Bakers for our bread and rolls. In those days they weighed the loaves of bread, and if the bread was underweight they would supplement the difference by giving you a portion of mince. This had a thin layer of sugared pastry on top, a bread pudding-like filling with another thin layer of pastry underneath. We never objected to running errands for a loaf of bread as there was always a piece of mince handed over that was eagerly devoured before the bread reached its recipient. Our meat was obtained from Tommy Halesworth, who always had a beautiful array of all types of cuts of meat in his windows. The road had two cooked meat shops that sold tripe, pig's trotters, brawn, often with the pigs bristles still sticking out from the meat and aspic jelly, pressed beef, luncheon meat, sweetbreads, brains; in fact every piece of offal that came from an animal. They

81

were very popular with the locals because they were much cheaper than the regular butchers. Our grocers was the Maypole, an off-shoot of Lever Brothers who also owned the Home and Colonial, another similar grocers seen in the East End. Tins of Goats Brand condensed milk, margarine and cheese were bought here. Billy Adair had a seafood stall quite close to Kelly's pie and mash shop, and boys being boys we used to sing out, "Billy Adair, Billy Adair, all balls and no hair." Billy was of course bald, a heavy set man and a former wrestler, and the boys took advantage knowing full well that Billy couldn't leave his stall to chase after us! Our shopping expedition usually finished up with grandma buying me a packet of wine gums for my good behaviour!

Come Fridays, it would be bath night in the scullery. The scullery had bare brick walls whitewashed over, a stone floor, a bare roof-tile ceiling with a small glass skylight shaped the same as the tiles, a ramshackle shelf holding pots and pans, a copper in one corner, a stone sink in another, and a gas stove. The scullery door led into the yard, its walls whitewashed to reflect light into the kitchen. A galvanized tin "bungalow" bath, when not in use, stood out in the yard, upside down on top of the mangle. Our bath water would be heated in the copper, and as the water in the bath got colder, a saucepan of hot water would be added. We took it in turns to bathe in the same water according to seniority; I, being the youngest, was always last. Grandma would put soda in the bath and use soft brown soap that she brought home from Shell Mex used for scrubbing. The towels for drying were not real towels at all; they were old laundry bags that had seen better days and were never water absorbent; the cloth just slid over your body leaving your skin covered in fibres. Your face would be reddened by the soda. By the time it was my turn to bathe, the water would be tepid and a film of scum had formed on the surface. My grandmother was never gentle when washing you, the face flannel was literally smacked into your face, the soft brown soap rubbed into your hair then rinsed off by having a saucepan of cold water thrown over your head!

If ever grandfather took a bath, my grandmother would open the yard door so that the cold air would blow in directly on to his back, standing back unseen in the frame of the kitchen doorway laughing her head off! The comments from my grandfather were never exactly polite ones! A normal wash was never referred to as a wash; it was always a "rinse" or a "sluice".

There was never any instruction given on personal hygiene at home; it was something you learned along the way and observed from others whom you mixed with. It was a long road to go down before you became completely knowledgeable and understood bodily cleanliness as it should be. I think my grandmother just never had the time to explain or show us how or what you should be doing.

The scullery had a small inner window ledge where ointments, toothbrushes and toothpaste were kept. One evening when my grandfather was preparing to go out, he picked up a tin that he thought was Brilliantine, and mistakenly applied the ointment, Wintergreen, to his hair. Wintergreen ointment was used for general cold symptoms; it has a strong medicated aroma. He could not quite make out why his hair did not have the smell of flowers from the Brilliantine. We kept quiet when he went to his local in Bethnal Green Road smelling like a chemical factory! We never heard if his drinking partners had made any comments! On another occasion I was so hungry, I ate part of Winnie's cake of toothpaste! "Gibbs" was the brand name; the toothpaste came in little pink cakes inside a tin, and the peppermint smell appealed to me so much that I simply could not resist nibbling away!

There was very little room in the place we called the kitchen; I don't know why it was ever called a kitchen as it held no kitchen cabinets or appliances. There was never anywhere comfortable to sit, the room had hard wooden upright chairs and each door would be piled high with jackets and coats. It was a wonder that the weight of the clothing on the doors never pulled them off their hinges!

From the hall, or passage as it was known, you stepped down into the kitchen. It had a fixed dresser and a handmade side-dresser built, I think by my grandfather at some stage. If you happened to sit by that dresser you had to sit bent over or hit your head. The only one who could sit there unaffected was our grandmother, who was just not tall enough to be inconvenienced. There was a small cupboard built into a recess by the door of the coal cupboard running under the stairs. We had no "easy" chairs, just plain wooden ones; there was no comfort at all. The room had one window facing out onto the yard, the daylight curtailed by a brick wall belonging to the adjacent property.

A single gas light stood out from a bracket. Grandfather used to sit quite close to the gas light, and from time to time the gas mantle, made of very fine gauze, would start to disintegrate from the constant burning of the flame and release its snow-like particles on to our grandfather's head! We found this very comical while he sat there with his newspaper cussing and blinding. The fireplace had a small black oven range and fire grate. About the only thing that oven was ever used for was to melt cheese for our breakfast, bake an apple, or a rice pudding. There was an entrance door into the yard that was never opened.

We always had a caged canary or a budgerigar perched above the wireless, and every bird we ever had was called "Joey". There was also a very odd contraption that formed a shelf to hold the wireless. It must have been made by grandfather from two brass chains which ran down from the ceiling to support it. It looked most odd but no one dared to pass comment.

The wireless was our main source of entertainment; we would sit around in the evenings listening to *Monday Night at Eight O' Clock*, or *Band Wagon* with Arthur Askey. There used to be a favourite of mine with a chap called Sid Walker from the *Monday Night* programme; he was a rag and bone man who used to open with "Evening chums", then commence singing, ending with:

> Day after day
> I'm on my way
> Any rags, bottles or bones

Each week he would tell a different story, always of interest. We had "The Ovaltineys" with their own Ovaltine programme and song which we all knew. We became members and proudly wore the bronze-coloured Ovaltine badge. It could be most infuriating trying to find the stations at times, twiddling and turning the knobs to locate them. The wireless was powered by accumulator batteries, and when they were running low, we used to take them to a shop in Hackney Road for recharging. It was known as the Oil Shop, and sold paraffin and various other oils for domestic use and hardware. I disliked going there as it was always so dark and dingy and had the smell of oils about the place. During the weeknight evenings, with one or two of the aunts, we used to do crosswords or sing the songs from the sixpenny song sheets.

If some of the aunts were going out they would put their hair in curlers for a few hours, then heat curling tongs, either in the fire or over the gas ring. The iron would also be heated over the gas to iron their dresses, with the kettle steaming away to freshen up their hats. It was difficult not to be in any one's way in such a small space when all this activity was going on!

At bedtimes the aunts and uncles would retire. They did not possess nightwear of any description. The uncles slept in their underwear and the aunts in their slips. In winter in their unheated bedrooms it could be bitterly cold. It was not unusual to see my uncles sleeping with their socks on, and the aunts with scarves around them, going up the stairs to bed in their coats carrying candles! The gas lighting was never used in any of the bedrooms. We as children were not as badly off; we both wore Mickey Mouse pyjamas that opened at the rear which we called "trap doors". During the early years I had a period of bed-wetting. However much I tried to prevent it and save myself from being scolded by either Mother or Grandmother, it didn't stop until I was about six or seven years of age. Much later in life I discovered that it was a medical condition known as "primary enuresis"; night time bladder control. Both Mother and Grandmother were completely ignorant of this condition, and never ever dreamt of trying to find out its causes.

At weekends all the aunts would have a certain task in household cleaning. The whole of the dresser was stripped of crockery and washed; everywhere was scrubbed, swept and dusted. In grandfather's garden the multi-coloured marbled crazy-paving was washed. Even the windows were cleaned, and the yard scrubbed with a birch broom. Our house, although lacking in many things, did not lack cleanliness.

Our insurance man was a Mr Hicks, representing the Liverpool Victoria Insurance Company. He was an ex-army officer and a tall, well-spoken gentleman. He would be invited into our home to make his payment entries into the insurance books on our dinner table. His bicycle would be perched at the curbside, and after removing his bicycle clips, he would come in. He was one of the very few outsiders who were ever invited in. The younger aunts rather fancied him I think; their voices, although never a "Gor Blimey" accent, would suddenly become terribly affected whenever he paid us a visit! They even addressed my father, their brother-in-law, in the same manner. It was a natural instinct for them to behave like this whenever they were confronted by people who spoke better than they.

At Christmas, a pudding was made in a white enameled bread bin. Mixed fruit, dark sugar, flour and stout would be poured into the bin, and a silver "Joey", a tiny silver three penny piece, was dropped into the mixture for good luck. We all had a stir with a large wooden spoon and after a really good mix, it would be shaped into large balls, wrapped in muslin and boiled for a few hours. We would make paper chains from coloured strips of glossy paper, paste them together into a chain and fix them across the kitchen with balloons and a few manufactured decorations, although there were not very many of that kind. It was the one time of the year when we had chicken, which was a delicacy to us, and I looked forward to Christmas for the sake of the chicken alone!

Our front room or "parlour", as it was called, was the inner sanctum. Its door was always locked, and it was never used except at Christmas time, or if there was a family wedding. A party would be a gathering of my grandmother's sisters, their husbands, cousins and some of grandfather's friends. A primitive type of bar would be set up on the stairs, with a small wooden barrel of beer, crates of beer and lemonade, and a few bottles of spirits. The piano was about the best piece of furniture in the room, a richly colored walnut cabinet with two decorative brass candlesticks situated on the front panel, the piano keys yellowed with age. There were few pianists in the whole family and not very good players at that, and they managed with difficulty to accompany anyone rendering a song. Each year practically everyone partook in a song, or a monologue!

One Christmas whilst all the elders were in the parlour drinking and singing and singing and drinking, I sat on the stairs by the bar. I drank a glass of port, or perhaps a couple, finishing up falling down the stairs. My sister was the scapegoat, and got a good hiding for allowing me to get into that state. Another time I locked the parlour door when the party was at its height. No one but no one could get out, as the lock had jammed due to its infrequent use, resulting in everyone having to climb out of the front window into the street and re-enter the house again through the front door. I thought the whole thing funny; the party guests however did not.

There would be the same songs and the same monologues year after year. Uncle Tom would whistle one of Albert Whelan's popular songs, "I want to play in a big review." Aunt Jane who had a dreadful, nasal voice would sing "Franklyn D Roosevelt Jones" — "I've been told there's a new arrival in the Jones's family, yesireee, yesireee, yesiree-ee-ee." Grandfather would sing "The Rose of Tralee" or "The Mountains of Morn" and cry. He loved Irish songs, though why he should cry I never knew; he had never seen the skies of

Ireland. His friend, Ted Ferry, would sing "I had a Wheelbarrow that went round and round." My Aunt May regarded him as a dirty old bugger; he was always trying to grope her. Grandmother would sing, "Just a song at twilight." If anyone happened to speak while someone was singing there would be a cry, usually from my grandfather shouting "Order please, order," just as they did in the music halls.

There would be an intermission from the piano playing and singing; ham, corned beef and cheese sandwiches, sweet pickles and pickled onions would be passed around, hardly fine cut and more like doorsteps, but the bread was fresh so there was never any complaint. Grandfather would normally finish up drunk and had to be put to bed. We could hear his ranting and raving as he lay on his bed. The party guests would ignore it all and carry on partying.

One year when we were very young my sister and I were invited to participate in a party piece we had learned at school. She was the patient, I was the doctor. When I was supposed to say "Let me feel your pulse", I inadvertently said "Let me feel your parts". The whole room burst into laughter and I ran out of the room in tears for having been laughed at. I really didn't know what I had said that could have been so funny.

Uncle Harry would sing old East End songs that I guess were almost Dickensian. I often wonder how many of the true old East Enders are still around that remember any of these old songs that could, and should, have been placed on record for all time:

Bash me again Bill, Bash me again,
You caused me no heartache, you caused me no
    pain,
You called me a flirt and a flirt I'll remain,
You bashed me last night Bill, so bash me again,
He comes down our alley he knocks me about,
When ever he does so you'll hear them all shout,
But still I love him I can't deny it,
I'll go with him wherever he goes,

Everyone would join in on:

Come round any old time, make yourself at
    home
Put your feet on the mantle shelf,
Open the cupboard and help yourself
The meats in the oven, the bread's on the shelf
If he doesn't eat it, I'll eat myself
We don't care if your friends have left you all
    alone
Rich or poor, knock at the door and make
    yourselves at home.

When *Me and My Girl*, the musical with Lupino Lane, was showing in the West End of London, one of the songs from the show "Doing the Lambeth Walk" became an instant hit. It was sung everywhere, not forgetting the East End parties who brought it into their parlour repertoire. "Doing the Lambeth Walk, Oi" was invariably included into a sing-along. Other songs that resulted in a "knees up" would be "Knees up

Mother Brown" or "How they going to keep them down on the farm / After they've seen Paree."

Come the weekends, my grandfather would go out. Hardly a weekend ever went by without him coming home drunk. It was a way of life with him, as indeed it was with many other men. We accepted this and grew up with this around us; it was the norm. At times he would fall down in the hall and had to be helped to bed. Sometimes there would be terrible arguments between my grandmother and him when he came home in that state. There were times you dreaded him coming home knowing what was in store. He could be quite violent and at one time broke my grandmother's arm. We could hear the screams, my mother and sister ran down the stairs to her aid. Weekends could be very unpleasant. Why women stuck with men who made their lives so miserable is hard to comprehend, but leaving the home was out of the question. The song "Bash me again Bill, bash me again" just about sums up the East End women's philosophy of those days; they did not run away.

They had a saying, "You've made your bed, now lie on it." Grandmother could be rather canny. Whenever Grandfather was going out, she would turn the clock back one hour to reduce his drinking time. She referred to his drinking as his "suction"; he never checked his pocket watch, just observing the time by the clock on the mantelshelf.

Grandfather had once been a Hansom cab driver, and we used to have a photo of him wearing his livery — he was then a smart, good-looking man. He then became a dock worker for the next forty-five years. If ever you asked him for a direction, he would give you a route by naming pubs and who the brewer was to verify you had the right pub. It would become something like, "Go down the hill, you'll see the Queen's Head, it's a Truman's House. Do a right at the top and you'll come to The Good Hope, that will be a Taylor Walkers House . . ." and so it went like that, rarely by names of the roads. My father would have defined it as "the fine art of tavernry". My grandfather would clean his boots and shave the night before, and repair his boots if they so required from an iron boot hob we kept under the dresser. Apart from a dock accident, I never knew him to have a day off work. He was working in the docks when they had to fight for work to unload a ton of sugar at sixpence a ton. He crushed his thumb on one occasion and was unable to work, so I had to go with his book down to St Katherine's Dock for him to be "bomped on" to claim his sick money. Work clothes, protective clothing, overalls and the suchlike were not around in those days. They went to work in old clothing. In the winter overcoats would be worn, and he would come home at times with his coat soaking wet, weighing a ton from the rainwater it had gathered. The garment was placed over the fireguard in front of the fire to dry. The steam that rose from the coat smelt of the stale cigarette smoke from pubs and buses that had impregnated the cloth. Other than an interest in a newspaper, I never saw him read a book throughout his life. There was no quality of life, just work and the pub at weekends. Like my grandmother they never had a holiday between them.

Grandfather was known to us when we were very young as "Paba". "Paba" belonged to a Working Men's Club in Pollards Row. It was his regular haunt. My grandmother called it "The 'Ole" as the "Men only" bar was down in the basement. It was often my duty to go and get him out of "The 'Ole" to come home for his Sunday dinner. I would climb the stairs to the entrance hall to be met by two of the club's officials who would shout down into the depths, "Bill Cunningham down there?" which of course he always was. I would be given permission to go down to the bar. Behind it in a large glass cabinet was a display, of gleaming silver sports cups and trophies from both past and present events. "What does she bleeding well want now?" would be his remark, nearly always the same. He would proceed to buy me a large glass of cola, quite different to the American version of today, and sit me on one of the raised benches to watch men playing billiards while he finished his drink with his friends. The coloured billiard balls would hold me spellbound; the colours were so vibrant on the green baize under the low hooded lights. When he had finished drinking we would walk the short distance home together. He would sit down to his dinner alone in silence, and then go to his bedroom for his afternoon siesta. After his afternoon sleep he would have his tea then prepare to go out for the evening again.

We were sent to the Jewish grocers for his Sunday tea, either to Mickey Nemko's in Pollards Row or one other in Old Bethnal Green Road and the corner of Jew's Alley. Mickey Nemko's shop was completely disorganized; you entered into semi darkness and tins, cartons, bottles and jars were all over the place. He hardly had enough room to work from behind the counter with the stacked boxes around him. Mickey's knowledge of hygiene was very limited; you would see him put his hand in a barrel of pickled herrings, never washing or wiping them before serving you with the next order. Most off-putting to see was the sticky fly paper hanging from the ceiling with a host of houseflies and bluebottles stuck to it. He had a good clientele and people bought from him unconcerned about his lack of hygiene and his habits. Normally we would have to get grandfather a Dutch herring or a brown herring. The brown herring was placed in a small earthenware bowl and immersed in hot water from the kettle; it smelled and tasted revolting. How he ate it I shall never know.

The club had an ever-present odour of stale beer that hung permanently in the air. On some Saturday nights, they would have "turns" or acts in the club's mini music hall style theatre. The seats in the hall were thin, covered in red rexine, studded with round brass headed upholstery tacks. Behind each seat in every row was a shelf running along its full length with a metal guard where you could place your drink while you applauded, without fear of the glass falling down. Each turn would display a large placard giving you the name of the act! They were run very much in music hall style. Men would bring their womenfolk and children, if they were old enough, to see the show. We looked forward to going there on these particular nights.

The club arranged a pantomime each year for its members' children. For us, it was one of the highlights of the year to see *Aladdin* or perhaps *Puss in Boots*. We were given a bag of fruit and chocolate or sweets and a three penny piece; it was wonderful. The colours, the music, and the singing captivated us.

In the summer they arranged a coach outing for all the children. We loved these outings to Loughton or Theydon Bois, they were only parts of suburban London, but we used to think they were miles and miles away. The days were always sunny and hot, I can never recall having rain on any of the days. The coaches would be lined up outside the club, the children's excitement building up! The coaches or "charabancs" as they were then known, would be the Grey Green Coaches of Albert Ewers. We would be given an apple, an orange and a three penny piece as we stepped on to the coach. There would be a sing-song all the way and much merriment between us! The appointed area had a small fairground with a helter-skelter, a large wooden tower with a chute descending around it for sliding down its length on a coconut mat. Under a large marquee, tables were laden with sandwiches, blancmange, fruit jellies and cakes. A photographer would be present at these events to take your picture; little tinny efforts that would gradually fade after a time. Many of us would get stung by wasps that always seemed to accompany us to these outings. The St John's Ambulance was always on hand to attend to us. I once needed treatment for a large splinter I got from sliding down the helter-skelter, and a wasp sting on the backside!

When tea was announced, there would be a mad scramble for the marquee to get a seat. Wasps were everywhere: over the jams, over the cakes, over the sandwiches. Through the whole of the tea we would be half eating and half driving away the wasps. There would, of course, be more work for the St John's Ambulance people attending to stings. But it was a glorious day out and we could hardly wait for the next year's outing to come around!

Newspapers at home were the *Daily Sketch, News Chronicle, Reynolds News* and the London evening papers *The Star* and *Evening News,* and others brought in by the rest of the family. On Sundays, grandmother would hide the *News of the World* in her bedroom lest we saw anything she might disapprove of. Normally we would get around to reading it, and there was never really anything in the articles that would destroy our morals or put us on the wrong road! We were street-wise at a very early age. If there happened to be something of a sexual nature she would say "That's lust my child." The subject of sex was never discussed, it was a topic that was shoved under the carpet. Also never mentioned was any girl who had had a child out of wedlock, as she would be considered a social outcast. It was a dreadful stigma, and divorced people were also looked on very much the same. They were two taboos that the East Ender viewed as something dreadful.

Some afternoons, quite by chance, we might come home early, and we would catch my grandmother lying down on the floor in front of the fire, having made a comfortable bed for herself under a couple of coats, reading one of the cheap romance magazines, *The Red Letter*. She hated being caught in this situation. She would tell you that she had "just lain down" and "hadn't stopped all morning" — not that anyone resented her resting whatsoever.

Every week I would have to take the bag wash. In the winter she would wrap a scarf around my head secured by a safety-pin under the chin and send me with a hired wheelbarrow or pushcart to the Gas, Light & Coke Company in Whiston Road. Through the gates of the gas works you purchased tickets from a small office requesting the number of bags of coke you wanted, and then took them to where a workman stood shoveling coke into the bags. He took your tickets and filled the sacks. I would take the sacks of coke first to my Aunt Jane, who resided in Hackney Road in a Georgian house that I loved and which was initially the home of my great-grandparents. It then housed my Aunt Jane and her family. It had such a long front garden, a basement and rooms on three floors. Her daughter converted the large ground floor rooms into a hairdresser's salon. Aunt Jane would give me a copper or two, and I would then take the remaining bags to my Aunt Becky in Norah Square. As Aunt Jane was nasal in her speech, Aunt Becky had a slight impairment in hers. She was also a little more generous in parting with her coppers, so I always gave her preferential treatment.

Grandmother never had coke in the house; she always had coal delivered by Thomas Lebon's. The delivery was by horse and cart; coalmen carried the sacks of coal into the house on their backs, wearing a leather-type helmet with a leather covering running down to the small of their backs. The coalmen nearly always got a hard time from my grandmother who would berate them for the previous delivery of being nearly all coal dust and small lumps! I think they must have dreaded coming to our house, as indeed did any builder. They would have the same treatment. The money collected from my aunts was my cinema money, plus a few little extras.

With so many of us living at No. 74, it was a wonder there was no queuing for the toilet, situated outside the house! What a cruddy place our toilet was! Distempered plastered walls flaking away from the dampness, an iron cistern with a pull chain and a scrubbed wooden pine seat that went from wall to wall — it could never be raised. There was no such thing as toilet paper; old newspapers would be placed at the side of the seat for you to tear off. Some of our neighbours went to the trouble of cutting their newspapers into convenient squares and placing them on a nail, but not us; I suppose there was too much cutting involved. At Christmas time a supreme effort might be made to place a toilet roll there for guests' use. More time was spent in there reading newspaper articles. Uncle Alf would request comics to give his backside a laugh! At weekends, it was in regular use from our grandfather's imbibing. The smell from his drinking had a defined odor that became so familiar to us come Sundays. We hated it but had to put up with it until that brewery stench had disappeared. Even today if we search deeply enough in our minds, we can conjure up that awful, unforgettable smell.

Our garden, if one could call it that, was a small patch of earth and was the one thing that my grandfather would take an avid interest in. A small picket fence, painted green, divided the yard from the garden, and the earth had been paved over by small wedge like shapes of various coloured marbles. There were three flowerbeds; a rectangular one either side of the garden, and a centre circular bed, bordered by triangular pieces of white marble. It had a green painted trellis arch stretching from side to side, and a small wooden windmill with a little man at the side who would turn the windmill handle when the wind blew. Alexander roses grew in abundance on the trellis, and wall flowers, lilies, peonies, marigolds and a host of other types of flowers flourished. I would play out in the garden amusing myself catching caterpillars, spiders and flies, and doing horrible little things; pulling the wings off flies, and the legs off spiders, dissecting the caterpillars and placing them in an old "Mortlake" wax milk carton half filled with water, watching the results of their torture and final demise! The garden was overshadowed by a wood yard called Cripps, named after its owner. Our cats spent most of their time there and would only emerge when they were called for food. Cat's meat was the bill of fare for them on most days, plus any other scraps that were left over from the table.

100

One cat was named George, an unusual name for a cat, the other Blackie on account of his black fur. George was my favourite. He was quite old with grey fur and black tiger-like stripes. Because Blackie was not my favourite, I gave George lots of stroking and affection. For reasons unknown, my grandmother didn't really like him and was not particularly nice to him. If they did their business in the yard, she would put pepper down and rub their noses in it. Dear old George, I found him dead one day in the wood yard.

You could never be ill in our house, it was not allowed. No matter how ill you felt, you just had to carry on until it came to bed time. A doctor was never called; most of our ailments were treated at home with old wives' remedies and ointments such as Wintergreen, Germolene, Thermogene, Bella Donna plasters, Linctus, Fry's Balsam, White Horse Oils, Camphor Oil, and Union Jack Chilblain Ointment that came in tiny little tubs. One day Winnie was in bed with, I think, tonsillitis. She was sitting up with a slice of burnt toast soaked in vinegar on her neck tied with a scarf, one of my grandmother's old wives' remedies. How effective it was we shall never know, although Winnie did get better. Being the more refined member of the family she looked completely out of place. For grandmother's personal medicines she would send us to The Old Maids, a chemist in Bethnal Green Road. It is still there today, under that name, though I doubt very much if it belongs to the same family. You would collect the medicine and tell the dispenser that the last lot was not as good as the previous one; little did our grandmother know that they were just changing the colour of the same thing! She would tell them that she felt much better when the blue medicine was given instead of the red! Winters brought on chilblains, chapped hands and legs, coughs and colds; it was a common sight to see women with red, mottled legs from sitting in front of the fire too long. Fry's Balsam was often used for our colds. We had to sit under a towel with our heads over a pudding basin breathing in the fumes of the balsam. If you had a chest cold you would be rubbed with camphor oil or white horse oils. There was never any form of heating in the bedrooms, they were freezing. Nor was there any gas light, we went to bed with a candle. Chamber pots were placed under the beds; we called them a "po" or a thunder jug. Sanisal disinfectant was always placed in the bottom of the chamber pots. I remember one night, grandmother had been overgenerous with the disinfectant, so when I got up in the middle of the night for a pee, I found my testicles had accidentally dipped into the Sanisal! I was unable to sleep for most of the night, with my testicles on fire!

Grandmother's maiden name was Biggs. She had five sisters and one brother, Joe, who died prematurely from being gassed in the First World War. Aunt Jane remained in the lovely family home in Hackney Road, and Rebecca, whom we called Aunt Becky, lived in Norah Square, Bethnal Green. Aunt Sarah lived in Clapton, and aunties Francis and May lived in Barking. We liked visiting our aunts in Barking. The married surname of Aunt Francis was Fitzgerald; it sounded so aristocratic. I used to think that if ever I were to change my name, Fitzgerald it would be. They lived in nice suburban-type homes and at that time Barking was considered to be a very attractive area. In their early days, when they all lived together in the family home in Hackney Road, the sisters were feather curlers. The curling of feathers was quite an art. Feathers were always used on the fashionable hats of the day.

Grandfather had two brothers, Harry and Arthur, and one sister, Charlotte. Harry died prematurely, Arthur was a docker like Grandfather and Aunt Charlotte's husband deserted her and went to Canada. Aunt Charlotte worked as a cook for Allen & Hanbury's close by. We would visit the aunts as a matter of duty and respect from time to time. Aunt Charlotte lived in Finnis Street in Bethnal Green. Her home was like walking into a piece of Victorian history; glass cases of birds, animals and artificial flowers everywhere, heavy drapes and gloomy. Whenever you called on her you could guarantee she was always cooking something, and you had to sit down and eat. She had a strange habit when talking to you of picking at your neck. A very weird sense of affection! When you left you were guaranteed to have a pink neck!

Behind Shoreditch Church, famously included in the nursery rhyme "Oranges & Lemons", stood the Mildmay Mission Hospital. We went there for all our dental treatments, the main reason being that you were never charged. Sometimes you perhaps put a few coppers in their collection box instead. They made it a point of encouraging you to say prayers prior to having any work done on your teeth. I recall, despite having a raging toothache, having to partake in prayer and feeling pretty sure that the way I felt, the Lord was not receiving my prayers loud and clear! After prayers, you were led into the dentistry section. Gas was the method used to anaesthetize you. A rubber mask was placed over your nose and mouth and within a short space of time you awoke to find the tooth extraction over and you were being led out, semi-conscious, by the dentist's assistant into a room and put to sit at a large table. Gradually you began to focus and would see five or six other people, sitting around that same table, small, white, blue-rimmed enameled bowls in front of them spitting out the gunk from their mouths following their tooth extractions.

At a very young age I was in the Children's Hospital, later changed to The Queen Elizabeth's Hospital for Children in Hackney Road. It was virtually opposite our street. I was only there for a short period, as there was something wrong with my knees and I was unable to walk. The smell of that hospital always scared me. It represented pain, or pain inflicted by a nurse or doctor. My stay was rather pleasant in fact from what I remember; crisp, clean white bedsheets, a comfortable cot, bread with butter, and for the first time in my life I tasted Marmite. It took me ages to find out what they had given me, the taste was something I never forgot. If it was a sunny day the nurses would wheel you out onto the balcony looking down into Hackney Road. Family and friends were able to wave to you. Literally all the boys and girls in Bethnal Green went there at some stage or another. An expression used at home if you were seriously ill was that "you were on the gate". I never quite worked this one out, at least not for a long time. Grandmother loved to say to people, if someone she knew was seriously ill, they're "on the gate". Actually it meant that the patient was in intensive care, but at that time, the term "intensive care" was never used or even heard of. She was always concerned that if ever my grandfather got knocked down in the street, he hadn't changed his underwear. She feared the embarrassment, as indeed did many women in the East End. The very thought of your husband being knocked down and not having changed his underwear for over a week just didn't bear thinking about!

Come the early part of winter, London would start to have fogs. The fog would begin white and damp in the early morning and by evening would develop into a "pea-souper" — a dense yellow fog, you could taste its sulphuric tang and it was thick enough to cut with a knife. Visibility became so bad that you could hardly see your hands in front of your face. Coal burning from industry and people's home fires were the contributing factors. Many elderly people died during these times, the pungent, polluted air choking them. It was not until twenty years later that Parliament enacted the Clean Air Act, after 4,000 Londoners had died, spurring the government into action.

One sight gone forever, but the recollection of which brings back happy memories, was to see the night watchmen in their huts at a road works or a building site. Red lanterns were placed around the work area as cautionary signs. You would often see a brazier burning with the night watchman cooking his meal over the fire, sausages sizzling away in the frying pan. Now and again you might be lucky and be given a sausage. On most occasions they would be happy for your company to relieve them from the loneliness of the night. Most of the streets comprised of tar block surfaces, and if the night watchmen were not that vigilant, tar blocks would rapidly disappear from the site for the fire at home. They burnt beautifully but spat the tar out all over the place.

CHAPTER FOUR

School, Church and Choir

Practically all the boys and girls in the street attended St Peter's school, a Church of England school affiliated to the Church. It was a well run, disciplined school with good teachers. Our flag, King, and country were held in great esteem. We started at the age of three and remained there until we were twelve years of age. My earliest recollections were being in the primary class; it had a large dapple-grey rocking horse that I loved riding on; the memory of that horse has never left me. It was some sixty years later that, with my sister and cousin, I paid a visit to our old school which was still standing, and now an organ-makers' establishment. A lady came out while we reminisced in the playground, enquiring what we were doing there. We informed her that many years ago it was our school. She was very gracious in showing us around all the classrooms that we had once sat in. We came to the primary classroom, and I happened to remark that this was where a rocking horse I loved as a child was situated. I described it in detail and to my surprise and joy, she told me that her

107

sister now owned it! It felt good to know that the dapple-grey had survived the ravages of time. We felt that our school was extra special to us.

The caretaker, Mr Loft, known as "Lofty" was a heavily moustached, large, kindly man who wore a brown felt trilby whenever he entered the playground. He would ring his large brass hand-bell calling us to school, sometimes allowing us to ring it. We would then line up in our respective classes and enter the school. Our teacher would call out our names from the register, marking down those present and absent. Absenteeism was almost unheard of; the prospect of the school board man coming to your house was feared. Our Headmaster, Mr Thomas, used to park his car in the playground next to the house of Mr Raymond, the choirmaster. We boys loved his car; it was like an American gangster's, similar to those we used to see in the *Crime Does Not Pay* series. It had a soft-top, yellow coloured "plastic" windows, although plastic wasn't around then, I guess it must have been celluloid or some other substance manufactured at the time. We would jump onto the foot boards, moving his chromium headlamps like searchlights, playing "cops and robbers" crying out, "Calling all cars, calling all cars." I don't think Mr Thomas ever came out and remonstrated with us; he was a very kindly headmaster. In fact, I cannot recall any of the teachers at St Peter's being unpleasant; they were firm but they were fair.

We were frequently visited by a nurse who would comb through our hair for nits; we called her "Nitty Nora", though I do not recall any resentment felt when her visits came around. She would stand there in her dark blue uniform and white cap, dipping the silver metal comb into a small blue-rimmed enamel bowl filled with disinfected water and comb through our hair.

A short prayer was said every morning before the commencement of class and our lessons. Normally we had one subject in the morning, changing to another in the afternoon. Once or twice a week we would have school drill which involved exercising in the playground outside. We wore coloured bands worn diagonally across the upper part of our bodies and formed into groups. I always tried to select my favourite coloured band, alternating from red to blue to green depending upon my colour preference at the time. The exercises were shoulder, arm, leg and body movements; time permitting we would have the game of O'Grady. You followed to the order of "O'Grady says". If you made the movement, and O'Grady never said it, you were out.

In the junior classroom you made a point, if you could help it, of never sitting with Edna Hoskins. She was always peeing herself and stank constantly of urine. If the teacher so ordered you to sit next to her, you suffered in silence. This also applied to Horace Andrews, who we called 'Orrie; as a small boy he used to wear brown velvet trousers with two pearl buttons either side. He always stank; he was constantly messing himself, and during summer time if ever you had the misfortune to sit next to either of them, it became an endurance test; you did your very best to try and keep

109

your mouth shut tight to prevent breathing in the fetid odours.

Our swimming classes took place at Haggerston Baths, a good fifteen minutes walk from the school. We would take swimming costumes, which we called "cossies". These were usually a two-tone affair made of cotton. The colours always seemed to be an orange top and black lower half which we purchased from Dunne's the Drapers in Hackney Road, for about three and a halfpence. The "cossies" were rolled up into the towel and placed under your arm. We were formed up in pairs and marched from the school to the baths. At that time we had a rebel in the school, who was never out of trouble of some sort, named Frankie Walker. At the baths, in order to enter the main bathing pool one had to walk through a small shallow pool known as a slipper bath. Frankie, for reasons known only to himself, refused to use the slipper bath which angered our teacher, Mr Desborough, to such an extent that he slapped him all around the slipper bath. During the whole of that scuffle and those whackings, I never saw Frankie shed a tear — he was a tough little sod.

One of the highlights of the year was Empire Day. We would proudly display our Union Jacks and march around the playground to music and songs. The large map in the school indicated every country marked in red belonging to the Empire. The red made up practically two thirds of the world and we were very proud. Everything was red, white and blue. The green lawn behind the church would be opened up for this special day to extend the activities, egg and spoon races, sack races, relay races, drinks and cakes on large wooden trestle tables to be consumed by an ever-hungry horde of school kids. If ever you asked one of them at school what they had for dinner, they would reply, "meat, 'taters and greens" regardless of what meat it was or what type of vegetables they had eaten, it was always the same reply. Every school kid's favourite dessert was jelly and custard; if you ever asked what they had for "afters", we never ever used the word dessert or sweet, it was not in our curriculum, if it had happened to be jelly and custard, they would rub their tummies in a circular motion of sheer delight. On Monday mornings you handed in your milk money for the week; the milk was delivered in silver-topped half pint bottles, together with a straw, and was drunk in the morning. From the silver tops and the straws we would fashion small spears and throw them at each other when teacher wasn't looking. Come the winter we would place our milk bottles close to the large combustion stove, so by the time we had our break the milk would be nice and hot.

It was King George V and Queen Mary's Silver Jubilee in 1935, and every schoolchild received a china mug with the pictures of both King and Queen in an oval framework surrounded by draped flags of the Union Jack and Royal Standard. In 1936 the King died. I recall standing with my grandmother listening to the funeral commentary over the wireless, and even at a young age I was quite moved. In 1937 George VI became King and we were all handed a coronation beaker with the pictures of King George and Queen

Elizabeth with the initials "L. C. C." (London County Council) emblazoned beneath. This was followed by a street party, with the street decorated with flags and buntings, a sea of red, white and blue. Trestle tables were erected and joined into one huge table where we all sat. Piles of sandwiches of fish paste or cheese, jam, cakes, buns and jellies were placed on the tables together with lemonade and tea. On sitting down, the food was rapidly demolished. It was the most wonderful thing ever. East Enders were a very patriotic people.

Invariably, boys being boys, we would fall down in the playground and graze our knees. Every other boy seemed to have a scab of sorts on their kneecaps. Their jersey sleeves and jacket sleeves at the cuff were often shiny from the mucus being wiped from their noses. Parents could not afford handkerchiefs and tissues were not around then, so the poor boys used the only method they knew to wipe their noses there was just no alternative.

Trousers were held up by snake belts which were two-tone and elasticized, boots were bought from Wickams in the Mile End Road or Gammages in Holborn. I never got to wear boots until called up for National Service. I just wanted to be like the other boys, but my mother made me feel very much out of it by making me wear patented Cromwellian shoes with silver buckles that left me open to unkind remarks and ridicule from the other boys. In the summer we liked wearing plimsolls, light on the foot and as we firmly believed, you could run faster in them. Many was the time where I had to sneak by my grandmother so that she could not see me wearing them. I was not allowed to wear them in the street.

Another fallacy was that if you peed on a lorry's tyres, it would go faster. At every opportunity when we saw a lorry parked part hidden from public view, we thought that we were doing the lorry driver a great service by having a pee on his tyres!

Emptying out a boy's trouser pockets was like emptying his treasure trove: a catapult, a Jew's harp or a mouth organ; if you didn't have a musical instrument of sorts, a comb and tissue paper would suffice; as well as marbles, string, penknife, and a lucky charm.

It's funny how certain things stand out in your memory. I recall being in class when we had to read out essays we had written. One boy named Lenny Davis, a tall, thick-set, blond haired boy from Warner Place, was asked to read out his essay. He commenced reading, "My dad is a dustman and goes to the beer pub." I pondered and thought why did he make the comment about his father in public? Why should he let it be known that his father drank? Why the words "beer pub," and not public house? "Beer pub" was the term often used instead of pub or public house, but to write it down as such did not seem quite right. This was my first experience of becoming critical, though I never recognized it as such at the time.

My sister became infected with scabies, a horrible disease that left you itching and scratching, day and night, gradually developing into sores all over her body which eventually turned to scabs. She believed it was caught from swinging on the toilet doors at school.

Scabies is a highly contagious disease that quickly spread both to me and my aunts, May and Winnie. The family had great faith in St Bartholomew's Hospital (Bart's) in Smithfield. We visited there for both examination and prognosis. Aunt May must have given permission, not really fully understanding what we were about to experience, as we were paraded before a whole class of medical students. The next thing we knew, we were all undressed and led into a lecture hall, totally starkers on a platform, staring out at forty to fifty students, while the lecturing doctor pointed with his stick at the sores on our bodies! I felt very uncomfortable and embarrassed not only for myself but for my sister and aunts at being exposed like this. It seemed an eternity standing there while a banter of questions and answers bounced between the doctor and his students. It was a great relief to us when the ordeal was over and we were allowed to dress and go home. Our ensuing treatment was to have sulphur baths at a clinic in Russia Lane, behind the Bethnal Green Town Hall. Russia Lane at that time had a notorious reputation for thieves, cut-throats and squalor. The squalor was most decidedly there, the reputation of having thieves and cut-throats was unfounded. The name Russia Lane and the square at the side of the Town Hall, Patriot Square, were the names given, no doubt, by some very Leftist councillor who had been brought up on a diet of Communism, revolutions, Marxism and Lenin. The name, so close to the leafy Victoria Park Square and the library, never quite befitted the surrounding area. Names of a more serene nature, rather than revolutionary ones, would have been more apt.

The school organised a Country Holiday Fund. For a small sum, underprivileged children could take a holiday in the country. I started to save my pennies, religiously putting them away each week into a china basin in a cupboard in the kitchen. Shortly before I was about to go away, my money went missing. We never knew who had taken the cash. I was absolutely distraught. The family somehow got together and saw that my holiday did not go amiss. I went to Harwich from Liverpool Street Station with 'Orrie Andrews; we stayed with a fisherman and his family. He would take us out in his rowing boat to fish. 'Orrie and I went out one day and got stuck in the mud. Fortunately before the tide came in we were rescued and never went near the mud flats for the rest of the holiday. I loved the smell of the sea, the smell of the seaweed washed ashore in black and dark green heaps lying across the pebbles, and we loved to pop the little pods of the seaweed, looking for small crabs and picking up interesting sea shells to take back home to London as a memento.

On school holidays our grandmother would say, "I put my hands together the day you go back." She dreaded them as it would entail our being at home for a certain length of time, which would upset her routine. We boys would form into our little team and go to the parks. Victoria Park was the grandest and our favourite park; we called it "the Vick". Leaving our street we would trek along Hackney Road to Cambridge Heath,

115

crossing the road into Bishop's Way, then on to the park. We would invariably make up bottles of lemonade from the yellow lemonade crystals that dissolved in tap water, shaking the bottle to give it a fizz. Stopping off in Bishop's Way, we would buy a bag of broken biscuits. I would always try to pick the ones with the pink icing on the back, or ask for any stale cakes as these were always cheaper. Victoria Park had a magnificent wrought iron gate you passed through, with a stone statue of a dog, which we understood had saved someone's life from drowning, as you crossed over the Regent Canal Bridge.

The park had a large boating lake and an island in the middle with a Chinese pagoda that you could reach by bridge. You could hire a boat to row, hire a skiff if you were a good oarsman, or take the larger motorized boat that would give you a tour around the lake. We would sit by the lake, drinking our jaundiced-looking fizz, eating the biscuits or stale cakes and feeding the crumbs to the ducks and swans that would come to you if they saw you were eating. We would remove our shoes and socks and paddle in the lake for a spell. The park, so prolific in trees and greenery, was a happy escape away from the streets. It was wonderful just to walk across open fields where all sorts of activities took place. It boasted a Lido where we would occasionally go and swim and sunbathe. We considered going to the park an exciting adventure. Other days would be divided by going to London Fields which had a large pond. We didn't like going into that water; it was said that bloodsuckers lingered there.

One day I fell into the pond and returned home soaking wet. My sister got a walloping for allowing me to fall in! Our other park ventures nearer home were Ion Square and Piggy's Island. These parks were just tiny open spaces with swings, seesaws and a roundabout. It was not unusual to fall off of these leisure contraptions and go home with a bump on your head or a grazed knee.

At about the age of eight I joined the St Peter's Church Choir. Choir practice was twice a week, our choirmaster and organist was Mr Raymond. He was quite a martinet and would stand no nonsense. On two occasions I was dismissed from the choir. I cannot recall the actual reasons but suspect it was for larking around during practice or some other misdemeanour. On the second time of being thrown out I cried all the way home. One of my aunts, Aunt Winnie, took me back and pleaded with Mr Raymond to reinstate me. He succumbed and I was back in the choir. On Sundays we would change into our cassock and surplice, with fresh scrubbed faces and hair parted looking like little cherubs when, in fact, we were quite the opposite. In procession we would enter the church, ascending the three stairs to the altar, pair off to be seated in the pews directly opposite the church organ. Mr Raymond had a small mirror facing him, and as he played he would look into the mirror to see if we got up to any antics during the service. Our delight was if there happened to be a choral wedding as we would be paid a shilling. Out of this we would have to pay for our own white high stiff collar and small black bow

117

purchased from Dunne's the Drapers. The cost of collar and bow was a penny and three farthings. When we were handed that shilling after a wedding service we felt like millionaires. We could then afford to buy a bar of Double Six chocolate from 'Arry Orseye's. This was a chocolate bar with twelve sections of differently filled chocolates, ranging from strawberry, coffee, caramel and other flavors, or perhaps one of his freshly made ham or cheese rolls, or even a Doubleday's steak and kidney pie. That shilling meant the world to us!

At Christmas time we choirboys, accompanied by Mr Raymond, would go around the streets clothed in our cassocks and surplices singing carols and making a collection. Money from the upper floors of houses would be thrown out into the street, and it would be our task to run around picking up the coins. We thought nothing of retaining a few coppers for ourselves and giving the rest to the church; even at that age we had learnt to charge a commission! At the end of the singing we would be invited to his house in the school playground for hot blackcurrant cordial and mince pies. It was his way of thanking us for our efforts.

When I was about twelve years of age the vicar at St Peter's church informed me that he could find no records of my baptism. I was always given to understand by my mother that I was christened there. Our vicar decided to take matters in hand and promptly baptised me at the church font with 'Orrie Andrews as my godfather. Much later in life, it proved to be very hard to understand that 'Orrie, a boy we had grown up with, turned out to be different; not interested in girls like the rest of us. There were signs, even at an early age, that his interests were not quite the same as ours, but we were too young to recognise it.

The church had a hall in Warner Place, St Peter's Hall, which is still standing. We enrolled in the Cubs. It was a junior version of the Boy Scouts. We "dib, dib, dobbed" and our Cub Leader was called Akela. It was another world. We wore green pimple caps with yellow cord, our scarves were plaited blue and yellow held by a leather toggle. We felt very proud of our outfits. Most of the "pack" had names of the animals from Rudyard Kipling's *Jungle Book*. I loved the activities and hearing about the animals from his stories. It was a great institution that taught us many values. The girls enrolled in the Brownies, the junior body of the Girl Guides. There would be functions and concerts from time to time in the hall when both Cubs and Brownies would share the evening.

Each week I would pay a visit to the library. The books and the selection of subjects opened up a whole new world for me, I would spend hour upon hour there quenching my thirst for knowledge and broadening my horizons. It introduced me to Rudyard Kipling and Jack London's *Call of the Wild*, never realizing that later in life I would be standing in the very places that Jack London wrote about. To buy a book or to be able to afford one was out of the question. Thank God for those libraries. I became a member and recall going into one of the smaller sections which contained an electric fire. I had never seen one in my life before and became terribly curious as to how it worked. Poking my fingers up behind the elements I was thrown by the electric shock to the other side of the room. Might I say from that moment on I never tampered with electric fires again.

The walk to the library, along Bethnal Green Road via the Salmon and Ball public house, housed a secret that I never knew for many years. Outside the Salmon and Ball public house two men were hanged for participating in the Spitalfields Riots of 1769. One was John Doyle (an Irish weaver), the other John Valline (of Huguenot descent). The riots were actually centred to the east, and were put down with considerable force.

The Bethnal Green library building is close to the original village green, now Victoria Park Square. The building erected by the green was Blithe Hall, recorded in an eighth-century document. Taking the toll over the years of different accents and bad handwriting, by the fourteenth century it had become known as "Bleten Hall Green". Another hundred years on, Samuel Pepys recorded his journey to "Bednall Green". Behind the library, a large mansion was built called "Bednall House", by a rich merchant named John Kirby, which eventually became known as "Kirby's Castle" by the villagers.

In 1727 the mansion was turned into a private asylum for what were then classed as mental patients or "lunatics". The original building stood until 1843 when it was demolished. A new asylum was opened in its place and existed until 1920, before being closed to make way for a housing estate. Its inmates were transferred to Salisbury.

My grandmother used to tell us that when she was little, she used to see the inmates in the grounds, making faces behind the wire fencing at whoever looked in. It was known to all of us, and is still called, "Barmy Park".

CHAPTER
FIVE

The Early War Years

On 3 September 1939, war was declared. It was a glorious Sunday morning, just like a mid-summer's day, the sun was shining and the azure sky cloudless. Halfway through the morning, the warning siren sounded, I think, for the very first time. It was the first of hundreds of times we were to hear it over the next five years. Mr Irons, the proprietor of a newsagents and tobacconist shop at the corner of Gosset Street and Kite Place, came running up the street with great difficulty; he was grossly overweight, wearing a tin hat and gas cape, with a wooden rattle in his hand. The rattle was to be used to alert people if we had a gas attack. Mr Irons was in the ARP and looked extremely worried, as if the Germans had already landed.

Grandmother, on seeing Mr Irons running up the street, dressed as if he was about to go "over the top" from the trenches, started to have a panic attack and screamed almost to the point of being uncontrollable. I took her back into the house, sat her down on the stairs, and calmed her back to her normal neurotic self!

THE EARLY WAR YEARS

People began to be issued with gas masks; these were skin-tight against your face so that when breathing out they would quiver and make sounds like a flatus (fart).

Babies' masks were like a space capsule called the "Mickey Mouse." With their bare legs protruding, many babies were frightened at being placed in these capsules and would scream their heads off. Gas masks were carried in small cardboard boxes that we tied with string and wore over our shoulders; we carried them everywhere. Homes were provided with either Anderson shelters or Morrison shelters. Grandfather would have none of it; he was not going to have his garden dug up for an Anderson shelter! So we became one of the few in the street who did not have one.

Barrage balloons started to go up all over London. They reminded me of huge silver elephants without trunks. The Committee of Imperial Defence authorized an initial barrage of 450 balloons for the city's protection. During the Blitz, 102 aircraft struck cables, resulting in sixty-six crashing or being forced to land. The best example of these "balloons in combat" occurred during the V-1 offensive against London in 1944. They proved an integral part of the air defence system and in this case formed the third and final line of defence against this low-flying weapon. Approximately 1,750 balloons were amassed from all over Great Britain forming the largest balloon curtain in history. Although guns and fighters destroyed most of the V-1 bombs (1,878 and I,846 respectively), balloons were credited with 231 "kills". That was the last "hurrah" for British balloons when the war came to a close in 1945.

The blackout began two days before the war commenced. Blackout rules were enforced and everyone had to cover up their windows at night with black material. Street lamps were turned off, so people walked the streets in total darkness. Some had nasty accidents, walking into walls, falling down unlit staircases and walking into the canals and ponds. There were several fatalities, particularly through road accidents. It took quite a while for people to become accustomed to the darkness. In the homes, families were putting up blackout blinds and curtains. They got used to turning off the lights before opening a window or door. To expose your home with any light showing, you would hear a cry from an ARP Warden shouting "Put that bloody light out!" Practically everyone carried a torch; they bought "No. 8 Ever-Ready batteries" regularly to keep the torches powered. Strips of brown paper were stuck on windows in a diamond pattern to prevent shattering from bomb blasts. The blackout was intended to make it difficult for German bombers to find their targets. Each week in the *Hackney Gazette* people were being summoned to the courts and fined for not keeping their premises in total darkness.

The Ministry of Food instituted a rationing system. Who would have believed that it would remain for fourteen years until it finally ended in 1954? We would register with our local shops and were provided with ration books.

On 8 January 1940 bacon, butter and sugar were rationed. This was followed by meat, tea, jam, biscuits, breakfast cereals, cheese, milk, eggs and canned fruit.

One of the few foods not rationed were fish and chips. The scarcities created by such strict rationing led to the black market. There was hardly a thing that was not rationed. People were deceived into buying horse meat, thinking it was beef. As the war progressed, clothing was rationed on a points system, as was petrol. It became a black marketeer's paradise. If you had money, you could buy anything. This was the birth of "the spiv".

The average standard of rations was:

1lb 3 ozs meat
4 ozs of bacon or ham
3 pints of milk or 1 packet of milk powder per month
2 ozs of butter
2 ozs of margarine
2 ozs of fat or lard
2 ozs of loose tea
1 egg per week or 1 packet of egg powder per month
(1 packet making the equivalent of twelve eggs)
2 ozs of jam
3 ozs of sugar
1 ozs of cheese
3 ozs of sweets
2 lb of onions (onions were rationed between 1942–1944)

These amounts were per week, unless stated

In the second week of the war, Aunt Eileen married her cousin Harry; both were Catholic and had to obtain special permission from the church to marry. Winnie, with a work colleague and my sister were bridesmaids, and I was selected as page boy. No suitable shoes could be found for me, so urgent improvisation was required which resulted in my sister having to give up a pair of her shoes, which were then painted in a metallic bronze to match my page boy outfit! The wedding arrangements were brought to a halt as I refused to budge until I had a buttonhole flower like everyone else! My mother was shouting and becoming quite hysterical. I tore the bronze coloured satin shirt I was wearing in anger! I was screamed at, shouted at, until finally a buttonhole carnation was found. I relented and the wedding proceeded without a hitch!

A few months went by in the "phoney war" period when the evacuation of children was implemented. Schools began to close down, and no longer did you see children playing, the streets were empty. Most of our playmates and school friends had departed for Somerset, Norfolk and other counties. St Peter's' school teachers and its children had gone. I never knew the reason why we were not included. Since there were no children I knew left around the neighbourhood, I started to befriend other boys and girls in the area where my mother had the café, who had not yet been affected by the evacuation.

We were invited to cousin Stanley's twenty-first birthday party above a public house in Brady Street. I can still see Stanley, with his black wavy hair and beautiful smile; he was a handsome young man. He had joined the RAF as an air gunner but was shot down in a raid over Germany; he was placed on the missing list for a long time, and eventually given up as "presumed dead". Two other cousins were to follow him — Charlie and Sonny were killed in the D-Day landings.

My mother had enrolled us into Ruby Bond's dancing school in Queensbridge Road; I was thrown out for having two left feet and returned to the streets! My sister Dawn became an accomplished singer and tap dancer and appeared in quite a few concerts. Clad in tartan, she would perform her song and dance routine of "McDougall, McNabb and McKay". I went to see her at the Excelsior Cinema. I was a little out of my depth at the time and didn't appreciate how good she really was, but her talent sadly was never pursued.

Things were beginning to happen in London. Official establishments were beginning to have sandbags placed around their entrances and at other weak areas, prone to blast. A group of us children participated in the war effort by filling up sandbags at Kingsland Road fire station. It was exciting and great fun but short lived. At that young age it was impossible to understand or comprehend what was about to take place.

Father was found to be unfit for military service and was directed to various jobs, some of which were quite unsavoury. Some of the jobs he was sent to were quite demeaning, and if he felt that the work was not for him he developed a ploy that prevented him from obtaining the position. He would be interviewed, mentioning to the interviewer that he felt it was his duty to tell them that he took things. The interviewer would say, "Well, how do you mean, you take things?" Father would reply, "I can't help it, I have this compulsion to take things." He never did of course, but it worked every time and the interviewer would politely say, "I don't think you will be suitable for this position" and Father was sent back to the Labour Exchange to re-register.

Having the foresight in what was to come, he found a small cottage in a village on the outskirts of Tring, in Hertfordshire, for 3s 6d per week and evacuated our grandparents and three aunts. The village of Wiggington was hidden away up in the hills on the fringes of the Rothschild's estate. They remained there for the rest of their days. Both Nan and my grandfather are buried in the village cemetery, and Father and my aunts are buried in Tring.

Over the years, I would go back there many times. Visiting my Nan's in the country was always a very welcome escape from Bethnal Green. Whenever one of my aunts invited me, I would jump at the chance. Aunt Enid was the favourite of my father's sisters, she was full of fun and laughter. We would meet at Victoria and get the Green Line bus to Tring. She used to make the most delicious sandwiches for us to eat on the journey. I used to think it was miles away, which of course it was not. It was fantastic to be away from the drabness of the East End, if only for a few days. Amazingly, there were people in the village of Wiggington who had never been to London. Some still adhered to folklore, such as if a single girl wanted to find a man, she had to place a "besom" (like a witches broom) outside the door!

128

I loved the bedroom I slept in at my Nan's cottage, old and countrified, with a sloping ceiling and a bookcase full of books. All the family read and the mobile library would call weekly at the village. Nan, even into her late eighties, would read on average six books a week and could relate all the characters in the books she read. Aunt Enid and I would get up very early and go into the fields mushroom picking and Nan would cook them with bacon. We also had fresh bread from the local bakery, everything tasted so wonderful! Nan would take me by local bus into either Chesham or Amersham. We would dine at a fish restaurant and her table manners were so ladylike, I loved her quiet reserved manner. Sometimes she would take me down the country lanes gathering cob nuts; she would hit the branches with her walking stick and I would do the picking up of the nuts. She was a magnificent cook, particularly her steak and kidney puddings. Grandfather would cut the cabbage and dig up the potatoes for cooking that day, no pesticides, just pure natural food that tasted out of this world.

The village had two pubs; although under age, I could sit with my aunts and have a glass of lemonade. Aunt Joan, who was an accomplished pianist, would play and Aunt Enid would mimic an East Ender singing in a "Gor Blimey" accent. One evening I bought a raffle ticket and completely forgot about it — the pub promptly informed me that I had won a cockerel! Taking home the bird, still feathered, Nan had my Aunt Lil pluck the feathers out in the garden, where I assisted in part, until it was made ready for the oven. Those were idyllic days!

CHAPTER
SIX

The Evacuation

We were eventually rounded up for evacuation. Neither our parents nor grandparents were there to give us a hug or a kiss goodbye, or to wave us off. We were tagged, labelled and shipped off by train like refugees from Euston Station and informed we were going to Bicester. I had never heard the name before. In fact I don't think any other evacuee on that train had heard of it either. I carried a small suitcase of clothing, that broke open on the train, spilling all its contents and which was beyond repair. The journey on that steam train seemed to go on forever; I remember the clickety-click over the rails. Lowering the compartment window by its leather strap to relieve the monotony of just sitting there. I poked my head out, only to receive an unsuspecting hardened speck of soot from the engine flying into my eye. I spent the rest of the journey attempting to remove the offending particle.

Bicester was a small agricultural market town. The main street was Sheep Street, at its heart. It had a population of approximately 20,000–30,000.

I returned to Bicester on a few occasions long after my evacuation days. To my sadness, the town has been

torn apart by a modern ugly supermarket and other
buildings erected in such a small area so that it has lost
its character. The cottage where we once lived, and its
occupants, like the decimation of the town, are gone
forever.

On arriving at Bicester, we were transported by bus
from the railway station to a school where we were
assembled, and the locals came to collect us. I was
never sure whether it had been pre-decided who would
have us, or whether they simply came along and
selected us by how we looked. I will never know. My
sister and I were separated; seemingly most of the
people did not want a boy and a girl together, rather
boy and boy, or girl and girl. I was paired up with a boy
named Lenny Ebbs from around the corner to us in
Bethnal Green. We were sent to a house on a council
estate on the outskirts of town; we didn't like the house
or its occupants and made a hasty departure back to
the school. We arrived back to an empty assembly
point; all the other children had been claimed.
Eventually a woman, a Mrs Baughan, and her son Jim
came along and took us a short distance from the
school to their home. The address was No. 3 Ladysmith
Terrace; a small row of flint-stone terraced cottages.
When we entered their home it was apparent that they
were as poor as we were. There was a small
low-ceilinged living room, with a dining table in the
middle of the room on which stood an oil lamp. Most
noticeably, there was no wireless. Candlelight was the
only other form of lighting in the house. The kitchen
was half scullery, half kitchen. An open staircase led

through to two open floor bedrooms. Husband, wife and daughters shared the first floor bedroom; we, with their youngest son, shared the room at the top of the house with a sloping ceiling. Lenny and I shared a bed. The toilet was in a shed way across at the back of the house where potatoes and vegetables from their allotment were also stored.

The Baughan family was an ordinary working class family. Mr Baughan worked with the GPO repairing outside telephone lines. The eldest son Joe was away in the Royal Navy, the eldest daughter Mary was in the WAAF's, and Jean was away in domestic service. Ray, the youngest daughter, was still at school, as was Jim, the youngest son; he was a similar age to us. They were a good-looking family; the daughters were all attractive girls, and as evacuees we got on extremely well with them all. I cannot recall having any disputes the whole time we lived there. After settling in and acclimatising ourselves to our surrounds, we reported for school. The school specialised in boxing and singing, and fortunately I was able to manage well in both subjects.

We were all assembled in a Methodist church hall and addressed by the head teacher regarding future arrangements for schooling. During his address I was rubbing my hand; I was called out in front of the whole assembly and caned six times over the palm of my hand for not paying attention! The school, along with its teachers and evacuees, had come from West Ham. After my caning I didn't hold this West Ham school in very high esteem! It was the first time that I had ever been caned. A suitable place was found to educate us, which

I loved, on the outskirts of Bicester. Bignall Park was on the fringes of the village of Chesterton.

Bignall Park was a lovely grey stone manor set in the most beautiful grounds. It was the finest building I had ever entered. All the manor's contents had been removed to make way for classrooms, leaving the beautiful paneled walls and polished wooden flooring that had become stained with writing ink from careless and thoughtless evacuees like us. Each school day we were transported by bus from the town square to Bignall Park.

Singing and boxing were given precedence over other subjects, and I happened to be chosen for both. The music teacher would take me aside privately and sit at the piano, with me standing beside her, practising the scales for a school production of *Aladdin*. Come the time nearer to the concert I backed out through fear. I was terrified at the thought of having to perform in public. Fortunately, there were no repercussions for not participating.

One glorious summer's day, the class was out on the terrace for singing lessons. We were singing "Do you ken John Peel." Part-way through the song, a hunt came into view, riding across the fields at full gallop with their hounds, hunters in hunting pink, to the sound of the horn. Quite apart from being a splendid and exciting picture, I could not think of anything more apt for that particular moment! The gamekeeper was often seen walking through the grounds with his shotgun, stopping at trees that housed crow's nests. He would shoot right through the nests, sometimes

134

blowing a crow completely out of its residence. Our main meal of the day was provided at one of the outer buildings which served as our dining room. Considering that rationing was in full force, with shortages of certain foodstuffs here and there, the school managed remarkably well. The food was adequate and not ghastly as school dinners often were.

Under the guttering of the building of where we ate, swallows nested. After lunch and before we had time to return to the classroom, I would sit and watch those lovely birds darting backwards and forwards, sweeping low and ascending high into the sky, diving, skimming the earth before soaring up again, and repeating the whole process over and over again. I could have sat there watching them forever.

We had a mobile shower unit visit the school regularly; it was set up like tents with canvas roofs and sides. We would line up, strip off, and ten to twelve of us would shower at one time. This was much better than having to bathe in a tin bath back at Ladysmith Terrace. The dentist would visit the school and literally everyone had a fear of his visits, as dentistry was nowhere near as sophisticated or technically advanced as now. In fact, it was quite primitive. To have a tooth filled or extracted was enough to put the fear of Christ into anyone.

Both Lenny and I became infected with scabies. For me it was the second time around. Mrs Baughan did not pursue professional treatment for us; she obtained the services of a woman who lived opposite us who made her own herbal ointments. We applied her ointment to our bodies and in two weeks the sores had disappeared. This was long before the general public knew anything about homeopathic medicine.

Boxing events were a regular feature on school sports days and fete days, which the town of Bicester would organise, our school being included. I did not particularly care for boxing, but you had to do it. Being left handed, always jabbing with my left gave me an advantage and I would gain more points than my opponent and usually finish up the victor.

The family's youngest son, Jim, would show us the ways of country life, taking us on numerous walks through the countryside, across fields and meadows, crossing and leaping over brooks and streams, into woods, fishing for minnows, collecting birds eggs, and teaching us the names of birds, flowers and trees. He showed us which springs were to drink from the crystal clear ice cold water tasted like no other water that had ever passed our lips.

We watched the frogs' spawn in the ponds and their development into tadpoles, catching them and doing some horrible things to them that even now I feel ashamed of. Those poor creatures! We enjoyed eating elderberries, gathering blackberries, seeing the bluebells in the woods, primroses growing wild, listening to the songs of the birds and the buzz of the bees. It all merged into one beautiful harmonious picture. The countryside evolved into an everlasting love that I became eternally thankful for.

Walking down a lane one evening on our way home, as darkness was just descending, I was with a group of boys and we were talking rather loudly about Germans and parachutists. I mentioned the police station keeping rifles. From out of the blue, a wartime sergeant constable appeared, wheeling his bicycle, looking every inch like a taller version of Barry Fitzgerald, the Irish film actor, and giving me a shocking telling off, quoting the "Careless talk costs lives" poster slogan. This was not to be my first run in with a policeman; I got a firm cuff behind the ear from a good old country copper for swearing on a Sunday, in the heart of town. I never forgot that cuff.

Since there was a shortage of hens eggs, we would go looking for moorhens' eggs. There was very little difference in taste. Rabbit and game were a regular feature on the menu at No. 3 Ladysmith Terrace. Mr Baughan had an allotment so we were fortunate enough to have plenty of fresh vegetables in the home. At that time I hated parsnips.

Mrs Baughan insisted on placing them on my plate and told me to eat them up. Craftily, when no one was looking, I would pretend to cough, grabbing a few at a time and shoving them into my trouser pocket. This mushy matter would harden and leave a coating on the inside linings. I used to empty the white-yellow gunge down the toilet in the outhouse.

Returning home at night, tired from the day's excursions, we would sit in the small living room, with the oil lamp glowing and casting shadows across the room. Mrs Baughan would give us a cup of Oxo and a slice of bread before sending us up to bed.

The other evacuee and I had different interests with regards to friends. He found his friends and I found mine. I befriended a Johnny Venner from Punderson Gardens in Bethnal Green. If anyone knew Punderson Gardens you would wonder where on earth the gardens came into it. It was just a street of houses. Johnny lived at the most prestigious address in the whole of the town, Bicester House, occupied by the town's most illustrious couple, Major and Mrs Coker.

The Major was the epitome of a British Army Officer; tall, erect, moustached, with a clipped military accent. The locals would speak of his wife as "Lady Coker". Whether or not she was a titled lady we never knew. She was a very attractive woman, always very friendly to us and forever accompanied by her two dachshunds, Roma and Romeo. Bicester House was a manor; the manor's stone walls surrounded two-thirds of the estate, with a spinney and brook at the extreme end of the grounds. My friend, along with another evacuee, did not live in the manor; they were accommodated in an outhouse quite close by, somewhat austere in its furnishings, but quite comfortable. The Major kept two large wooden chests in the outhouse, his rank and name painted on them. As inquisitive boys, on one particular occasion we rummaged through them, delighted to find belts of machine gun bullets, swords and various other items of memorabilia from the First World War. We simply played with them, returned everything back into its place and forgot about them.

138

Bicester House became a regular feature in my comings and goings, and I gradually got to know the servants of the manor. One day they invited me into their kitchen for tea. One of the maids, Olive, was having a boiled egg. It was the very first time I had ever seen anyone slice the top off of a boiled egg with a knife it intrigued me! I had so much to learn, both in table manners and etiquette. We did, at times, venture into the manor's living room; Johnny would remove a few cigarettes from the Major's silver cigarette box and smoke them, unseen, elsewhere on the estate. Occasionally we would attempt to crush the dried leaves from the trees, roll them in newspaper and smoke them, although not very successfully I might add! We were told to refrain from this as it would give you lumbago!

We played on the estate, running through the fields, down into the spinney, and climbing trees. In the walnut season, we scaled the trees for walnuts, removing the hard green skin; our fingers becoming yellow-stained as the nuts emitted their juices, releasing a smell like iodine. The Major and Lady Coker would hold fetes in the grounds; to us it was always an exciting event though we had hardly any money to spend on the stalls selling edibles.

Uniforms were beginning to appear around the town in numbers. Soldiers were being drilled on the asphalt road close to Major Coker's estate. We would watch them marching up and down to the orders of the Drill Sergeant, wearing forage caps and trying to keep them on their heads as they had not yet got used to wearing

139

them. Older men started to join the Home Guard and formed units; convoys of army lorries, Bren gun-carriers and tanks were driven through the town quite frequently. The RAF were very much in evidence too, there were so many airfields around us.

At this time, with the amount of aircraft seen in the skies, I took a great interest in planes and became quite adept at plane-spotting. I could identify a Wellington, Blenheim, Beaufort, Avro Anson, Airspeed Oxford, Hurricane and Spitfires, as well as Gloster Gladiators from Weston-on-the-Green, towing gliders, and also German aircraft. Returning home one afternoon the clouds were very low, and I heard the drone of an aircraft. By the sound of its engines I knew that it was not one of ours. The whistle of a bomb was heard, then an explosion. The air raid siren sounded immediately. The bomb had detonated in the village of Launton, a mile and a quarter away from us. Fortunately, no damage was done. It was to be my very first taste of the war.

Lord Beaverbrook, as Minister of Production, was asking women to give up their pots and pans. We would play our part in helping the war effort by going around the town collecting scrap metal; aluminium appeared to be on the priority list for helping to make Spitfires. It was a bonus every time we were given an old aluminium saucepan, and we hoped that we had gathered enough to build a Spitfire. The railings of churches, parks, and people's front gardens were removed along with tramlines in London. There was a real spirit amongst the people all helping with the war effort.

Bicester on Sundays was not my favourite day; we were made to go to church two to three times. Our place of worship was the Methodist Hall in Sheep Street; the preacher, Sydney Hedges, knew us all by name. We would go there in the mornings and again to Sunday school in the afternoon, to a class run by Blind John. In the evenings we would go to the chapel opposite and, if we were lucky, they would show a film. The whole town closed down on Sundays; nowhere was open. If the day was fine it was bearable, but if it rained it was a miserable place to be in. In summer we used to have a marvellous Sunday school outing on the river from Oxford to Abingdon. It was one of those memorable days that was essentially English, and how you would always like it to be.

The cinema was the place to take you away from the harsh realities, into another world. Bicester was blessed with two. One was at the far end of town, the other formed part of the Crown Hotel in Sheep Street, Bicester's main thoroughfare. Outside the Crown there would be cabinets displaying picture-scenes of the current film being shown. I remember looking at some with Ray Milland, secretly hoping that when I grew older I would look like him.

In the evenings the town was very active with uniformed personnel. Pubs were always busy, though you never saw any drunkenness, firstly because the beer was watered down, and secondly spirits were hardly ever obtainable.

In the little enclave where we lived, the local milkman, Mr Tuffrey, gave me the job of helping him out on his milk round. This was on a council estate on the fringe of the town. He drove a pony and trap, almost at a racing pace, leaning straight back and holding on to the pony's reins. I would quickly collect the jugs from his customers and he in turn would fill them from the large metal churns. I would then return the milk to the customer post-haste. I loved helping him! I felt like a charioteer alongside him in that trap! His wife, very much a country woman, large in stature, enormous arms and as strong as a horse, kept pigs at the back of the town. Effortlessly, she could carry a sow in those huge arms of hers and throw a half-hundred weight sack of potatoes over her shoulder as if it were nothing!

Very often I would accompany her and watch her cleaning out the pig stys and feeding them. I have always retained a fascination for pigs; I could watch their behavior for hours on end. It was my first experience in seeing a pig being slaughtered, which at a young age I found barbaric. The poor animal was hit hard on its forehead with a mallet, stunning it and then a spike was driven into its brain. It was strung up and cut all the way down its belly, with its entrails dropping out. A bucket was placed underneath to collect the blood draining from its body. The slaughterer placed his arm into the bucket of blood, moving it in a rotating motion and black pudding was then made with it. Finally the pig was taken down, laid on the ground, and straw spread over its whole body before it was set alight, burning all its bristles off. It was then removed to the butchers. That scene never left me.

The town had a small open air swimming pool that we frequented at weekends. I think all of Bicester's boys and girls must have attended there on the same day. It was here, unaided, that I learned to swim. The sense of accomplishment gave a great boost to one's self esteem, something at that age which made you feel very proud.

We were destined to be immunized in a chapel close to the town's main square. There were quite a few of us waiting to go in, sitting outside on a very low stone wall that was situated six foot above a stream. The wall's stone surface was extremely smooth and before I knew it, I slid backwards, dropping into the stream, cutting my forehead and drenching my clothes. Arriving home, I got a telling off for getting my clothes wet. It was the first and only time that Mrs. Baughan was ever cross with me — though I felt the reprimand was a little unjust.

In the fields close to the milk round an Italian prisoner of war camp was installed. They wore dark-brown dyed battle dress, with red patches sewn on. Some of the local girls became friendly with the prisoners — but how friendly I shall never know. My curiosity aroused such an interest that I started visiting the open camp. I sat with them around an open fire and spoke with them. I would ask them questions, and they would ask me questions. They showed me photographs of their families and girlfriends. One very pro-Axis Italian prisoner had made a ring depicting the swastika of Germany, the column and the axe of Italy, and the rising sun of Japan, all filed and shaped from a piece of aluminium. Other prisoners made the most inventive things from aluminium, metal, perspex and coloured toothbrush handles. I was impressed with some of the rings they made from the metal, inserting multi-coloured fine lines on the face of the ring from toothbrush handles. They would offer me coffee and sometimes wanted to share their food. They were, in most part, a friendly lot, longing to return home when it was all over.

Throughout my time as an evacuee, I only saw my father once. He brought me a Meccano set that I shared with the other boys in the house, making various models from the Meccano catalogue. My mother paid me a visit only once. Things got so bad that the clothing I had was wearing out. No letters or parcels were ever sent to me that I can recall. Through the school, they arranged for me to be sent to a woman who took apart a lady's old two-piece costume that someone had donated, making it into a jacket and trousers for me. It looked most odd; it was too narrow at the waist and looked too feminine, but there was nothing else for me to wear. I felt embarrassed to wear it and hated it.

Lenny, the other evacuee, was taken back to London by his mother. I had seen my sister only once; she was staying at the Fox Inn with a nice couple who moved away from the town, resulting in her being returned to London. After Lenny's departure I was left alone, until a few months later my grandmother appeared out of the blue and took me back to London.

My sister, having already returned to London, had made arrangements to meet my mother at her café in Haggerston. Dawn waited and waited for my mother; she went and sat in a shelter. There were several of these brick shelters in the streets that could accommodate around forty people. Families were already sitting in the shelter in readiness for the next air raid that night. Fortunately, with their foresight, anticipating a raid taking place, they were all safe when the German bombers came over and dropped a land mine quite close to the church on the other side of the road. Mother never turned up, leaving my sister in that shelter alone. My sister and I did not see her until the war was over.

CHAPTER
SEVEN

Back to London

Arriving back at No. 74, my grandmother made a bed for me on the floor in the parlour, alongside the piano. There was no more sleeping room in the house, so I slept like this for several months. My aunts' husbands were in the forces, so they had returned to No. 74 with their children. Eventually, I had my own bedroom for the very first time. It was the same room where I used to sleep on the floor with my parents and sister. The fireplace had a small black iron oven range and fire grate. I used the oven as my safe. It became a hobby going around the streets the morning after an air raid, and collecting shrapnel and silver metallic-backed black strips of paper, dropped by German aircraft to confuse our radar system. As fast as I placed the shrapnel in my "safe", Grandmother would remove them. She thought that they would explode!

Our grandmother and grandfather were left with the responsibility of raising us. Our parents, during their long absence, never provided anything for our support, financially or otherwise. We could have very easily been placed in a home.

The younger aunts felt resentment at having to help financially to clothe and feed us, and at every opportunity they would make this apparent. My sister was treated quite badly by them, and they used to taunt her, reminding her that we were charity children. If the aunts happened to be in conversation and my sister appeared, the talking would cease, and she was made to feel a social pariah. Nothing could be more hurtful at a young age, having no one to turn to, or a shoulder to cry on. It had an everlasting effect on her. Because I was a boy, and having so many women in the house, I was never treated in the same way, or if they ever did pass remarks like they had to my sister, they went right over my head. It's hard to understand how members of your own family could have been so cruel and insensitive.

Later in life, I have tried many times to analyse our family; summing it all up they were not a family as one would expect. They were never close-knit, each person seemed to go his or her separate way, devoid of love and harmony. I never saw any show of affection by our grandparents to our aunts and uncles, not even a hug or a kiss. They just didn't know how to express love, or any form of tenderness. My sister and I, being the youngest, were just an extension of the family. We too never experienced any love. The sisters, our aunts, could be bitchy, envious and even jealous of each other. It was only much later in life when I was the only one left at home that a very close bond developed between my grandmother and me.

From my period as an evacuee I had developed a slight country accent, so that when I teamed up with my old schoolmates again, I must have sounded to them like a country bumpkin. This left me open to some ridicule for a while. I enrolled at Teesdale Street School, as sadly St Peter's was never to reopen. Teesdale Street was a mixed school, with separate classrooms for boys and girls. It was at this school that we had two special teachers; the headmaster Mr McHarry who sang, and Mr King who played the piano. Classical music was introduced to us, with explanations of the pieces and composers by Mr King. It was never a boring experience and I have been forever thankful for it, in arousing our interest in music. The school had excellent teachers. Initially, I was in Mrs Jarvis's class. A lovely lady who always wore her hair in a bun, she was quite attractive. There was a period when sex education was introduced for the very first time into schools; by then we boys knew all the answers and there was very little that you could teach us! Out of devilment, I remember embarrassing Mrs Jarvis by asking her how the cockerel implanted its seed into the hen! The poor lady's face reddened and she had great difficulty in trying to give the answer! By the time she had finished fumbling and stuttering, it became as clear as mud! Even now, I feel sorry I ever asked the question! The school had a playground on the roof of the building, surrounded by high wire mesh fencing. Cricket and football were played along with general exercises and games. I recall St Paul's Cathedral being quite visible from here.

148

To get to school there was a shortcut through Hadrian's Estate. This was a council estate of grey-white brickwork, green painted doors, windows and balconies. The flats were fringed with back gardens, and a large enclosed garden was in the centre. We knew several families who resided there, with many of the boys and girls attending the same Teesdale Street School. Hadrian Estate had a caretaker, Mr Johnson; he was an absolute tyrant. If we were seen walking though his domain, he would chase us, shouting at us until we were off the estate. At times we would go to visit a friend, and if he saw you he would question you until he was satisfied that your visit was genuine. Mr Johnson was not very much liked by us, as he would scare many boys and girls who simply wanted to make a shortcut. One day passing through the estate, I happened to look down into a garden and saw something silver glinting; removing it from the soil, to my great delight I realised it was a half-crown piece; I had never possessed such a sum in all my life! I felt wonderful, I felt marvelous, and I felt rich. Making for the nearest shop en-route to the school, I stopped off at Mark Costa's. Marky, as he was known to us, was a small Jewish grocer and confectioner who reminded me of Groucho Marx, bespectacled with a moustache just like him! In harder times, we would fiddle this poor man with empty lemonade bottle deposits, returning a bottle, getting a penny back, and on the way out, removing two more empty bottles from the crates and taking them back the following day! On this particular day, with a half crown to spend, I bought bars of chocolate and sweets and shared them with some of my classmates.

There were many times when we went to school with holes in our shoes; we had to cut out cardboard and place it over them. If you had a "downpour" the cardboard would get wet and soggy, and you would have to wait until you got home again to tear off a piece of cardboard from an old shoebox to re-plug the hole. When our clothing got beyond repair, or too small to wear, Grandmother would take us down to the "Shallorams" in pursuit of something suitable. I remember looking with her for suitable shirts. We rummaged through piles of them on different stalls. She sorted one out for me that was pale blue with little silk star motifs and a frayed collar saying, "There that'll do you nicely for school." With great reluctance, I wore it to school, making attempts to hide the worn area as much as I possibly could by raising my jacket and looking as if my neck had disappeared!

Opposite our house, on the other side of the street, lived the Abrahams. After the blackout was lifted their house was illuminated all night by a lamp post situated immediately outside; it poured light into the front rooms of our house. The Abrahams were a most gentle and nicely spoken couple. We were never sure whether they were brother and sister, or husband and wife! We also never knew of the status of the young girl, Lilly, who lived with them. Rumour had it that she was an orphan, but she could have been their daughter for all we knew. They were very private people and we respected them as such. With the Abrahams, only brief pleasantries were ever exchanged, conversations never ever occurred.

The neighbouring Patterns, who lived a few doors away from the Abrahams, were below average height. Mrs Pattern was the same height as grandmother; they could easily have been mistaken for twins! Both of them loved the doorstep gossip and could always find the time to chat for hours about nothing. Very often we would hear "I'll just pop across to see Pattern" — the Christian name was non-existent. Connie, the daughter and my sister's school friend, seemed the same height all the time I knew her; she never ever appeared to grow! You were lucky if ever you saw the father; he would pass you in the street as if he never knew who you were. I'm not sure now if he was just plain shy, or he found it too much of an effort to acknowledge you.

There was a public telephone box on the outskirts of Hadrian's Estate, and a blue police box next to it in Hackney Road. The telephone had a button "A" to press so you could register your call and speak. The other button "B", was to return your coins if the call was not made. We used to stuff the opening slot with paper where the coins were returned. We would leave it there for a couple of days and then with a strong piece of wire remove the paper so that the coins would fall out.

Aunt Eileen and Uncle Harry had moved to Croydon, since his work was there, but Eileen came to Bethnal Green daily to work at the Lion Mills in Hackney Road. Grandmother also worked there as an office cleaner. Occasionally, I would go to help her do

151

the dusting and other little chores. One morning, she gave me some A4 paper to take home. Placing this under my sweater, I was walking home along Hackney Road when the paper fell from my sweater blowing out onto the main road directly outside a police box. A constable very kindly went out into the road and picked up the papers up for me. Duly thanking the officer for his kindness, I gave a sigh of relief when I got home. Dear grandmother was dismissed from her job at the Lion Mills for leaving puddles of water on the stairs. I think by this time, she was past her office cleaning days but she could not accept it. Eileen, at the finish of work from Monday to Friday, would collect Harry's dinner, which my grandmother made, and take it home in a saucepan all the way back by train to Croydon.

In summertime after school, we would race to the bridge in the Broadway, climb through an opening in the metal railings, take off our clothes while we were still hot from running, and dive immediately into the Regent's Canal, known to us as "The Cut". The water was dark green, and you could not see a thing beneath; it was quite eerie. From time to time, you would see water rats scurrying along the bank on the opposite side; it was even said that there were dead donkeys in the canal, although I never saw any! Boys would be fishing from nets, a small bamboo cane with a white piece of gauze serving as the net, jam jars at their sides to place their catch in. Other boys would be dragging the canal with the rim of a bicycle wheel, and sacking stretched across the wheel, which improvised as a dragnet. Barge horses would be walking slowly along the towpath pulling canal barges, the tow rope running slack and dropping into the water, then tightening and coming up out of the canal, water dripping with green slimy matter that had been floating in it. If you were to fall in that canal today, you would be placed in quarantine for forty-eight hours.

We used to go swimming at the York Hall baths several times a week throughout the year. The York Hall baths, as with Bethnal Green in general, have a long association with boxing. Daniel Mendoza, champion of England from 1792 to 1795, lived in Bethnal Green. In my younger days our Bethnal Green boxing hero was Arthur Danahar. Boxing matches and dancing were held there. It is still used today for professional boxing matches. £2 million has recently been spent in refurbishing York Hall, including a new gymnasium. We started to use The York Hall public baths frequently when we were older, rather than endure that awful tin bungalow bath back at No. 74!

At the kiosk in the York Hall you bought a ticket for a bath, towel and soap. The towel was hardly a bath towel size, and its texture was as rough as anything. The small cake of soap hardly lathered! The baths were in numbered cubicles, so if you got into the bath and found that the water was too cold, you would shout out "more hot in number nine!" or whichever cubicle you were in. The attendant would then come along and release the water from an outside connection, which then came gushing into your bath at such a pace, that at times it became too hot. You would then have to yell back "a little more cold!" Fortunately, most of the time you got the balance right! They had a small canteen/caféteria where you could buy cups of Oxo, toast and other little snacks that were always welcome after a bath or a swim.

Sometimes we would go "up the Roman" — the Roman Road market, where there used to be a shop by the name of Tolliday's. I knew of no other shop like it. It specialised in steamed suet puddings of every description. Our faces would be placed hard against their windows to see steak and kidney puddings, bacon roly-poly, treacle pudding, jam roll and spotted dick. Our mouths would drool at the sight of all this wonderful food; alas, we never had the money to buy anything!

Each week we would attend woodwork classes at Daniel Street, and the girls would go to domestic science classes on those days. On one particular day in class, I walked past a bench that a boy was working on. Suddenly, I saw a spurt of blood rising out of my sock like a fountain. He had knocked a brace and bit off the bench, and the bit had gone straight into the vein of my foot. The teacher applied some rapid first aid to the injury and, with the help of two boys, placed me on a wheelbarrow and wheeled me to the Mildmay Mission hospital! After treatment, I was wheeled home in grand style on the wheelbarrow, to the dismay of my grandmother. She hated anyone being ill or injured; she lacked empathy in such matters.

Our lessons were interrupted from time to time by daylight air raids. Our shelter was on the first floor. It was a cloakroom that had been reinforced with an extra brick wall on all four sides. Mr Ridgeway, our teacher, would produce his newspaper — the *Daily Telegraph* — and have us read articles from the paper until the "all clear" had sounded and we were able to return to class.

Every Wednesday, my grandmother would give me a note to take to school requesting permission for me to leave class early to get pies and mash for the family. The notes were never refused. Off I would go with an oilcloth-type shopping bag and a china jug for the liquor to Cooke's pie and mash shop in the Broadway, London Fields.

I used to carry about twelve to fourteen pies, with the potato mash and liquor. With regularity, the liquor would spill over my hands, the thick hot green liquid running over my thumb and the back of my hand. There was nowhere to stop and wipe that horrible mess off. I just kept going until I arrived home!

The Blitz was to last from 7 September 1940 until 15 May 1941. During the air raids we never went to the shelters. Some went to the underground stations at Bethnal Green and Liverpool Street, others to the brick shelters in the streets. Bethnal Green became the epicentre of the Blitz with bombings day after day. At the sound of the siren, a sound that made your stomach turn over, we would all go down to our grandmother's bedroom and sit around the bed having cups of tea until the "all clear" was sounded. Sometimes the raid was short-lived, at other times it would go on for hours. I think we found being together gave us comfort. We would listen to the bombs dropping, some getting quite close, and anti-aircraft guns would be firing away from Victoria Park, the ping of shrapnel hitting roofs and iron guttering. Some nights it became so very bad the house shook, other nights a little quieter. Many of the residents down the street were either in the ARP, Firewatchers, or AFS; many teenagers became ARP messengers on bicycles.

The Ministry of Home Security, in response to Herbert Morrison's appeal for more firebomb fighters, initiated a nationwide scheme for The Boy Scouts Association to act as fire spotters in their own district. The patrols consisted of eight boys with a patrol leader. Fire watch was compulsory for all civilians of both sexes between the ages of sixteen to sixty years of age. A part time service of the Civil Defence required forty-eight hours' service per month. Not to turn up for a fire watch would result in a fine.

Our local rag, the *Hackney Gazette*, that most in the East End referred to as the "'Ackney Gazette'", continued to report court findings and at times, even in the country's darkest hours, could be found to be amusing. A Mrs Minnie Winter, aged thirty-seven, of No. 34 Pollards Row was fined £5 for concealing a naval deserter for fifty-one weeks. "I didn't know he was a deserter," she said, "I met him in a pub." The paper also requested its readers not to write and address letters to Adolf Hitler — "The G.P.O. (General Post Office) is not able to deliver them for the time being".

Uncle Joe was in the AFS (Auxiliary Fire Service) based at Bishopsgate in the City of London. He invited me along to the station one day, showing me all the apparatus, the fire engines he drove, and best of all, I was allowed to sit down and eat with all the firemen! Firewatchers were armed with a stirrup pump and a bucket of sand, not very effective when practically the whole of the City of London and the East End were ablaze!

In mentioning Bishopsgate and the City of London, I feel that I should cite a former colleague, sadly no longer of this world. He was at that particular time a City of London policeman, based at Bishopsgate. Joe was a very tall man, as indeed most of the City of London policemen were. He was a loveable, charismatic rogue. His beat took him from Bishopsgate to Aldgate. The beat had seven pubs, and each night on duty, Joe would consume two pints of beer "on the house". If there happened to be a raid and some of the shops were hit and others damaged, Joe would arrange for a lorry to come along and remove the whole of the shop front, including the contents. If the shop fronts were chromium like the "Fifty Shilling Tailors", so much the better, they brought a better price and were easier to get rid of.

One evening on his beat, he came across a row of garages that interested him — he found one garage locked. With no further ado, Joe gave the padlock a hard blow with his truncheon and gained access. It was like walking into Aladdin's Cave! The garage was stocked high with black market goods; chocolates,

157

nylon stockings and a few hundred eggs. Joe very rapidly dispensed with the nylon stockings and chocolates, and then commenced marketing the eggs!

He knew of a Jewish club owner in Aldgate who was very eager to buy. The club owner, at his request, wanted to see the eggs. Joe took him round to the garage but the club owner almost had a fit as he discovered that it was his! Since the goods were black market he could say absolutely nothing. On another occasion, Joe was in one of the pubs on his beat having a crafty pint, and while downing it he could see out of the corner of his eye, his Inspector. Joe, quick as a flash, shoved his pint under his cape. His inspector walked over to him and said that he would like him to accompany him around a couple of blocks. Joe held that pint for the whole of the walk! On returning to the pub, the Inspector said to Joe, "I do hope that you haven't spilt any of that beer." Joe had the luck of the Irish!

At some stage when the air raids were at their height, we gave up going down into my grandparents' bedroom. It was decided that we would all bed down in the kitchen at night. Our grandparents, aunts Eileen and May with their daughters, my sister Dawn and I all had our allotted sleeping places. Grandfather was at the end of the room with his feet under the dresser, Grandmother and I were under the table, divided by the table's spar, my feet hanging over the end one. Aunt May and Sheila slept beyond me under the wireless and birdcage. Aunts Eileen, Brenda and Dawn were in the opposite corner; Dawn's head perched against the coal cupboard. If grandfather had gone out for the evening, he would return after we had all bedded down for the night, resulting in our having to get up to make room for him to find his sleeping position. Brenda, being the youngest, would pee over my sister in the night! Having no change of clothes, she would have to go to work the following day still wearing the soiled petticoat.

During one particular raid, we had an explosion so powerful in its force that it lifted me over the wooden spar of the table on to the top of my grandmother! My sister slept on, she didn't even hear the noise. The Oxford Arms, Jones's Dairy, and several other houses were hit and completely demolished. The site made way for an auxiliary water tank for the Fire Service, as indeed were many bombed out sites. It later became an allotment for a time, to which the Queen paid a visit. It was later cleared for prefabricated houses to be erected.

During the cold weather, my aunts and cousins would sleep in their pixie hoods — a hat that was quite fashionable during the war. One of my aunts christened it the "Pixie-Poxie Hood". It got so cold that on some nights they would wear a balaclava and mittens! The cold draught would blow into the room from under the coal cupboard and the passageway.

As the war progressed, most foods were rationed, with the exception of offal. Restaurants were exempt from rationing which created resentment. The wealthy could eat out frequently and extravagantly, supplementing their food. Because of this resentment, certain rules were put into force. No meal would cost more that 5s, no meal could consist of more than three courses, and only one of meat or fish could be served at the same sitting.

The London County Council established the Londoners' Meal Service in September 1940 as an emergency system, feeding those who had been bombed out. This became known as "The British Restaurant". By mid-1942 the L.C.C. were operating 200 of these establishments. In Bethnal Green there was one restaurant in the Children's Museum in Cambridge Heath Road. A V-1 flying bomb came down opposite the museum in 1944, and there was hardly a window left after that explosion. The other British Restaurant was in Bethnal Green Road, quite close to Brick Lane. A three course meal only cost 9d. Standards varied. I ate in both of these and it was dire. The soup was watery, the main meal bland and tasteless, the dessert ... well, on one occasion, I ordered jam tart and custard. The jam tart was a hardened, sweetened piece of dough served in a square, a razor thin line of jam running through the centre and the custard ladled on to the "jam tart" had the consistency of water. In fact it tasted like water. These British Restaurants were not my favourite eating places! The tastier meals were found in the ordinary cafés. Corned beef and spam fritters were regularly on the menu, along with a lot of offal dishes. One of my favourites was stuffed sheep's hearts with roast potatoes, something you rarely see on menus now. There was, of course, a general saying that if you asked for something not necessarily out of the ordinary, you would invariably be told, "There's a war on you know."

My grandmother used to rant and rave about the stringent allowances, wanting to "string up" Lord Woolton, the Minister of Food. "A cess on him!" she would say, meaning that he should have a cesspit dropped on his head. Much later in 1946, a new Minister of Food was appointed, John Strachey, whom she also wanted to "string up"! Among our rations, I remember having a tin of corned beef, dated 1917, some twenty-four years old. That tin was still edible, even after all that time! The cooked meat shops in Bethnal Green Road were a blessing, supplementing the meager food rations. Offal was not rationed, so we were able to extend the weekly bill of fare with tripe and onions, brawn, sheep's hearts, luncheon meat, pigs' trotters, and many other forms of offal. The only item in these shops that was hardly ever available was liver. Things got so scarce that one week there was no meat available, only corned beef. It was the first time we were to see our grandmother break down and cry. A vegetable dish was named after the Minister of Food, Lord Woolton — "Woolton Pie". Oddly enough people were much healthier then than now, and certainly there was no obesity.

Recipes from the Ministry of Food were advertised, and were the most uninspiring dishes one could ever imagine. Some were really awful. Characters were introduced, such as "Dr Carrot" and "Potato Pete" to encourage people to eat home-grown vegetables. "Eat more carrots, you'll see in the dark better," we were told. It was rumoured that night-fighter pilots ate carrots to see in the dark.

A white loaf of bread was no longer available. We were introduced to the "national loaf"; it was practically all grain. Supposedly a "brown loaf", the colour was nearer to grey. There was no other selection of bread and the "national loaf" stayed with us throughout the war.

Sausages were made in three grades, "A","B" and "C". After 20 January 1941, sausage grades "A" and "B" were prohibited and only grade "C" sausage was allowed. Grade "C" permitted a meat content of less than 45 per cent but not under 30 per cent. The maximum prices per pound of grade "C" were:

Beef 7d, pork 11d, Kosher beef 10d
Sausage meat: beef 6d, pork 10d Kosher beef 8d

Fruit such as bananas and oranges had completely disappeared; they were not to return until well after the war was over. Everyone was told to "Dig for Victory" and to grow our own vegetables. We boys made ourselves a vegetable patch in the garden of a bombed out house, "doing our bit". Posters were everywhere. "Is your journey really necessary?", "Careless talk costs lives", "Even the walls have ears", "A slip of the lip may sink a ship", "Dig for Victory", and "Buy national savings bonds" were just a few of the slogans.

Every Wednesday and Friday the *Hackney Gazette* would publish the court cases of shops fined for overcharging on food. Owen Brothers of Bethnal Green Road were fined £50 and £5 guineas costs for selling three eggs at 4¾d each, the real retail price being 3¾d.

The Home & Colonial was summoned for contravening the Jam Order (maximum price) for charging 1s 8d on a 2lb jar of raspberry jam instead of 1s 6d and for selling twenty-one 1lb jars of raspberry jam at 10½d instead of 9½d. The manager apologized to the court saying he misplaced the schedule as he was always at the butter and bacon end of the shop. All summonses were dismissed on payment of one guinea costs, it was an honest mistake! Albert Franks, butcher of No. 164 Ridley Road was summonsed for overcharging on two best neck imported lamb chops weighing 9 ozs, at 8d, when the price should have been 6¾d. The case was dismissed with one guinea cost.

Grandmother started to use her culinary skills and made a cake. The nearest description would be, "rock cake gateau" that we called "her quick". It weighed a ton! grandfather was sent up to the docks at Greenock with his brother Arthur, with a parcel containing a whole "bit of quick". Uncle Alf in the army and Uncle Harry in the air force up in the Orkneys were each sent the cake on a regular basis, and I was to receive them much later while I was doing my National Service in Germany.

We would clamber over the bombed-out houses, rummaging through remaining rooms, removing, above all things, medicine bottles. We once found the metal insert of a copper and poured all the medicines into it and lit a fire, boiling the liquid up until it was bubbling. We waited for something magical to happen. As budding make-believe scientists we expected to develop

163

some wonderful solution for mankind! Sadly nothing happened!

At odd weekends I would go and visit my Uncle Joe and Aunt Dolly in Clapton, by which time I had two young cousins, Jose and Valerie. I liked my Aunt Dolly a great deal. During one visit the air raid siren sounded and I had to spend quite a few hours in their Anderson shelter with my two young cousins until the raid was over. Uncle Joe and Aunt Dolly were to divorce; sadly we were never to see Aunt Dolly and our cousins again.

During these years the wireless used to play the songs sung by Vera Lynn and Ann Shelton, the music from the bands of Geraldo, Jack Payne, Harry Roy, Ambrose, and Victor Sylvester, the soft melodious voices of Flanagan and Allen, the monologues of the Weston Brothers and Cyril Fletcher. There were also broadcasts by comedians Rob Wilton, We Three: Enoch, Ramsbottom and Lovejoy, Tommy Handley's ITMA, and that wonderful routine of Rob Wilton's, "The day war broke out," in his slow, dry, droll delivery.

It was at this stage that each Saturday I would get a No. 6 bus to Trafalgar Square to visit the National Art Gallery. All the old masters had been removed to safety in Wales; they had, instead, paintings of artists from the armed forces. Most of these were of war scenes, of well-known high-ranking officers, admirals and generals. Bomber Harris, General Montgomery, Air Marshall Tedder, and Admiral Cunningham were all there, along with paintings of land battles, sea battles, paintings of dog fights, of ships, destroyers, cruisers and battleships,

Hurricanes and Spitfires. Every war scene that one could call to mind would be here. They were changed quite frequently and the National Gallery became my weekly Saturday venue. During the week, the National would hold gallery concerts, seating 1,500 people. American GI's were always hanging around Trafalgar Square hoping to pick up a girl. We used to approach them with "Got any gum chum?" and in most cases they would pull out a packet of gum and hand you a strip. Being handed a strip of "juicy fruit" gum, unlike our Wrigley's coated tablets of spearmint, was something quite different. Servicemen and women from all parts of the globe would come to Trafalgar Square sightseeing. I went to cross the road one day and a wartime constable took my hand to escort me across. I looked up and found that the man holding my hand was Wally Patch, the film actor. He was in so many British films playing character parts and I felt rather honoured that Mr Patch had held my hand.

I recall seeing airmen's faces burnt and scarred. Those very brave men were so badly burnt that they became known as the "guinea pigs". Eventually, some 600 "reconverted" men of sixteen different nationalities formed a group called The Guinea Pig Club. Sir Archibald McIndoe, then just plain Archibald McIndoe, the plastic surgeon, would send groups of fliers up to London with tickets to the theatre and night club reservations. As the Battle of Britain raged, some 4,500 airmen would be pulled out from the wreckage of their flaming aircraft. Many years later I was to meet Lady

McIndoe, a lovely lady who at that time was involved in charitable work in the Caribbean.

Every other person then was in uniform and carrying gas masks. The American officers looked so smart in their olive green jackets and beige trousers, as did the Australian airmen in their navy blue uniform. I would look at the insignias, divisional signs, ranks and flashes on the shoulders of their different countries. There were Poles, Czechs, French, South African, and New Zealanders; so many nationalities passed by. One Saturday I arrived at Trafalgar Square during a Victory Bond drive. Standing on a rostrum addressing the crowd was Ivor Novello and the actress, Roma Beaumont. I could not take my eyes off them; they were the most glamorous people I had ever seen! Ivor Novello had blue-black wavy hair, and was wearing a camel overcoat with a polka dot red silk scarf. Roma Beaumont looked absolutely stunning. After the drab war years, to see those beautiful glamorous people up on that rostrum was too wonderful for words! A young fellow approached me of a similar age with an autograph book and asked me if I had their signatures, which I had not. He then showed me their autographs. He invited me to accompany him to the Garrick Theatre in Charing Cross Road, where Michael Redgrave was appearing in "Uncle Harry". We waited at the stage door for a while and finally Michael Redgrave appeared. He gave me his autograph on a piece of paper, and signed the boy's autograph book. Some twenty years later, I was sitting in the buffet car travelling from Victoria Station to Bognor Regis, when who should be sitting next to me but Michael Redgrave! We got into conversation; he was on his way to Chichester where he was playing in "Uncle Vanya". I related the story of meeting him at the Garrick all those years ago. He asked me if I had seen the show, so I informed him that at that time I could hardly afford my return bus fare back to Bethnal Green, let alone go to the theatre which, of course, was absolutely true!

A newspaper agent in Hackney Road hired me for a paper round after I had first obtained permission from school. A medical was also requested, and it was found that I required dental treatment. The school, in the meantime would not allow me to work. Managing to get the dental work attended to, I had to be re-examined again and was found fit to work. Part of the news round involved delivering to a large council block in Pritchard's Road. There was a woman on the second floor; her flat was at the far end of the balcony. Each time I neared that flat, I used to wretch and gag my mouth, as the smell was appalling. I couldn't put her paper through the letter box quickly enough, hand across my mouth and pinching my nose at the same time. That lady got lightning newspaper delivery! Worse was yet to come on Sundays, when I had to collect the money and face her. Opening her door, she would keep me engaged in conversation, and it was unbearable. I had to keep a perfectly straight face, pretending that everything was quite normal, when all I wanted to do was to get away and breathe fresh air into my lungs! It was my worst delivery out of the whole newspaper round. I dreaded going there.

It was a relief to go to the cinema to forget the austerity of war, if possible, with its drabness and rationing. We were deluged with British and American propaganda films to boost our morale. Cinemas were showing *Night Train to Munich, Hitler's Children,* or *Confessions of a Nazi Spy.* If someone appeared in a German uniform on the screen, the audience would hiss like a snake, not just one hiss but several. If, in a scene, a German did something cruel, such as hitting someone with a rifle butt, one or two of the older men in the audience would shout out, "You dirty, rotten, German bastards." It became quite commonplace when visiting the cinema to hear hissing, cursing, and swearing whenever Germans appeared on the screen. The audience became so carried away. With films like *Mrs Miniver* however, a wartime family story, you were guaranteed to watch without any noises or remarks.

On Wednesday 3 March 1943 Bethnal Green suffered its Tube shelter disaster; 173 people died from a terrifying crush, as panic spread through the crowds trying to enter the shelter. The underground station was one of the few deep level shelters in the East End. Situated in a densely populated urban area, it had, at times, held 7,000 people and contained 5,000 bunks. Approximately 500 people were already in the shelter when the air raid warning sounded. It was 8.17p.m. At 8.27p.m., a terrifying roar was heard as an anti-aircraft battery fired a salvo of sixty rockets from Victoria Park.

This sound was unfamiliar, creating anxiety and panic as the crown surged forward, with only a twenty-five watt light bulb to guide them in the dark of

168

the blackout. The station's steps were wet and treacherous as it had been raining. A woman, holding her child, fell near the bottom of the first staircase. A man tripped over her, starting the whole tragic event with each person tripping over another, creating a human domino effect. There were many rumours flying around at the time. Some said that it sounded like the noise of a train going over the railway bridge at the Salmon & Ball; others said it was Dickie Corbett, an ex-boxer and his gang who stationed themselves around the Salmon & Ball. It was rumoured that Jewish people took all their jewellery down to the tube with them, and that the gang created the panic as a diversion to rob.

Despite the best efforts of rescuers, twenty-seven men, eighty-four women and sixty-two children died. Another sixty-two were taken to hospital. It had been alleged that the woman who originally fell had survived, but her daughter had not. Fearful that the news of such an unnecessary disaster would demoralise the people, the government ordered that both the location and the precise number of fatalities should be kept secret. There were boys and girls from our school who lost their lives on that dreadful day.

One of the boys in our class who died in that awful disaster lived in Mansford Street. He lived in the lower part, which housed tenement dwellings. One block, next to St Lawrence School, was Meadow Dwellings. That building depressed me each time I passed by. There were two flats on each floor; a toilet was shared between two families on an arched open landing, with an iron balcony facing into the street and cold stone steps leading all the way to the top. Between 1830 and 1898 there were many similar buildings erected in the East End to accommodate the poor; they were easily identifiable by their sombre and drab appearance. However, in those days the buildings must have seemed like palaces to the poor wretches who were transferred from hovels of poverty and squalor to clean and decent housing.

They must have seemed a godsend, the great benefactors such as George Peabody, the Guinness Trust, and Lord Rowton, who gave their names to the buildings they erected. The East End is indebted to Peabody, an American philanthropist who provided $2.5 million, an enormous sum at that time, for low cost housing for Londoners who had to be poor, of moral character and good members of society to qualify. Lord Rowton also founded and built the famed Rowton Houses with his own money. One was in Whitechapel, the other in King's Cross; a working man's hotel, providing a single bed in a cubicle, and a bath, for 6d per night. Most of these buildings have since been converted into private, luxurious abodes, and some demolished. To hear of anyone staying at Rowton House, you instinctively knew that they were literally "on the bones of their backside"!

St Lawrence School had reopened as a play centre which we attended in the early evenings. Here you could participate in cricket, football, gymnastics and art classes. I spent very little time on gymnastics, but an excessive amount on art. In the summer we played cricket. It was nice to be away from home and find a place with those facilities. In those days, sportswear did not exist; we carried out our gymnastics in the same clothes which we wore on the streets.

It was at this age that I started noticing girls; one girl in the art class whom I became attracted to was Betty Wright. She was blonde, hazel-eyed and had a lovely lilt to her voice which I found appealing. I sent her a note asking her if she would "go out with me". She replied on paper, saying "yes". I was elated. This marked the beginning of discovering that I liked the opposite sex. The sole company of boys would begin to wear thin somewhat in its appeal! The romance with Betty was innocent. We would meet, going nowhere but the play centre, holding hands with an occasional peck. After some time our innocent little romance faded.

Quite close to St Lawrence School was another, the Mansford. This was a secondary school that closed at the beginning of the war like many others in Bethnal Green. During its heyday it had a fine reputation. Our Aunt Winnie attended it. It later reopened for evening classes and as a restaurant for high tea. The high tea was first rate; it was my introduction to pilchards in tomato sauce and spam; it was far nicer than anything I received at home. I would go there whenever I could afford to do so. I continue to eat both spam and tinned pilchards to this day.

On the odd Sunday I would go and visit Aunt Noona (Ethel) who had by then divorced her first husband and remarried a very quiet agreeable man, "Uncle Sonny". They resided in Clapton. Very craftily my main purpose of visiting Aunt Noona was that she was such a wonderful natural cook. Her Sunday roast dinners were unsurpassable, my sister and I were never sure where she acquired this talent, because she most certainly never gained it from our grandmother. She would give me odd little jobs in the kitchen, like beating up the butter and sugar for her cake-making, a small price to pay for a wonderful meal. She was blessed in giving us two cousins, Mavis and Tony.

Like the other boys in the street, it suddenly became the craze for us to have bicycles. Not wishing to be left out, I badgered my grandmother until she relented and we both went along to a second hand shop in Three Colts Lane that sold bicycles. I selected one that, with a new coat of paint, would be fine. Agreeing on a price of 30s, I walked home with her and the bicycle absolutely elated. It did not take long before I purchased a small tin of paint and decided to paint it in a Cambridge Blue. Grandfather, in his supervisory role, watched me paint the bicycle out in the yard and was constantly telling me that I was "treacle-ing" it on. There's nothing quite like someone watching over you when trying to make a first class job. With the paintwork dried, I could not wait to get out on the street with the rest of the boys who would assemble outside the church and ride off to Victoria Park. The time taken from when we used to scooter there was next to nothing! The traffic around the junction of Hackney Road and Cambridge Heath Road, before entering Bishop's Way, could be a little scary, but the more you were on the road the more confident you became. The bicycle gave us a greater amount of freedom in that it enabled us to go further afield.

John Finch's Yard was in Mansford Street. I would sometimes go this way to school as a diversion from the regularity and monotony of the same old route. John Finch & Sons were carriers. They stabled some of the finest horses you would ever see in London, magnificent animals, beautifully groomed, which pulled only light goods vehicles. Their drivers always looked splendid in their livery. The horse-drawn vehicles and polished side lamps were always an impressive sight. Whenever they drove by, the sound was unmistakable; the fast rhythm of horse's hooves striking the road, and the rapid turning of the wheels. You felt compelled to look up and admire equally both man and horse. They would come out of the yard on to a cobble-stoned ramp, the horse's shoes creating sparks as they eased their way out into the street. Close by in Claredale Street was the blacksmiths. John Finch's horses were taken here for shoeing along with horses from other companies. The blacksmith fascinated me; I would love to watch him working. The striking of red-hot metal, the metallic ringing, cling, clang as the metal was struck on the anvil, shaping, and forming it into horse shoes, then filing the horse's hooves, the hot metal shoe being placed on the horse's hoof, sizzling and smoking into a miniature cloud. I adored the smell that arose when this was done! Finally, the blacksmith would hammer the nails into the hoof with such speed and dexterity it would leave me gazing in awe.

173

The war was now turning in our favour. I lay in my bed at night, listening to the sounds of our bombers flying overhead, on their way to Europe to discharge their loads. Each night the aircraft grew more numerous, until the sounds of the engines seemed endless, and it became impossible to sleep. Looking out of my bedroom window, there would be an armada above. It was a most wonderfully reassuring sight and sound, knowing that the chances of a German air raid reprisal would be remote.

CHAPTER EIGHT

The Teenage Years

The school years at Teesdale Street passed. We were still at war, and having reached the age of fourteen, it was time to leave and go out into the world. When the day finally came to leave, I cried. I was at a point where I was just beginning to grasp maths and English, and had really become attached to the school. We were given the opportunity to state what we would like to do; I did not have one iota of a clue. Most of the boys in the class opted for engineering and raised their hands; so not to be left out, I stupidly raised mine.

I was selected for a job in electrical and telephone engineering with the firm of H.H. Electrics Ltd, in Clerkenwell (Little Italy). My grandmother bought me a pair of brace and bib overalls, and a small attaché case which on my first day she packed with a stotty cake (a Tyneside flat loaf) given to her by a neighbour, Mrs Pattern, who lived opposite, and an apple!

Off I went out into the world. I was engaged at 15s a week, for a five and a half day week. My very first task was to push a builder's barrow with another boy, laden with heavy electrical equipment, from Clerkenwell to a factory being rewired in Holloway. We worked at this factory for a few months, experiencing a series of air raids from the V-1's (Doodlebugs). As soon as the air raid siren sounded, we would dash up to the factory roof which had an excellent view over London. We could see the flying bombs coming over quite clearly, the throb, throb, throb of their engines, with flames spurting out, suddenly coming to a stop and gliding down to earth, creating death and destruction. They hardly ever came in our direction. We were able to catch first sight of them as they flew over London, the explosions and the plumes of smoke rising up dramatically. Each time, we debated where we thought they had come down. We were rarely accurate in our guesses as they could be very deceiving.

H.H. Electrics sent me on numerous jobs in and around London. One in particular I did not like was in Park Royal. I disliked the electrician I was working with constantly addressing me as "Bill". In today's terms he would have been referred to as a "smart ass". He loved to give the impression of being superior, which, of course, he was not, sending me to do tasks that really I should not have been doing. We were re-wiring a machine shed and he had me climb up into the rafters to a fuse board that was quite old, where some of the old porcelain fuses had cracked and the whole board was live. I fell off the rafters on to a lathe that was turning and gashed my wrist. He neither reported it nor bothered to take me to have it seen to. Each day when we finished work he would have me carry a heavy wooden tool box to Park Royal Station, which was a considerable distance from where we were working. I was very pleased when I never had to work with him again.

The same boy I had worked with in Clerkenwell was sent with me to an establishment in Clerkenwell Green, The Uniform Clothing Company. The basement of those premises to us boys was like an Aladdin's Cave. It contained uniforms, helmets, holsters, swords, and all kinds of wonderful things that would appeal to any youngster. At lunch break we would start playing around with some of the articles. One day, we donned fencing masks and started fencing with very lethal swords. I lunged with a thrust at the other boy's mask, thinking that the wire mesh would protect him. Regretfully the sword went straight through and cut him just under the eye. Fortunately the cut was very slight. It certainly stopped any further playing around with swords after that event!

The company sent us to some very interesting places at times. Not far from Clerkenwell Green was St John's Gate. During the war, I do not think it was open to the public, but as a boy it held me enthralled working there. St John's Gate has a rich history of the Knights Hospitaller. It was a monastic order, serving the sick and defending the faith, and was built in 1504. It was once the entry to the Knights' English Priory. The museum today has the most wonderful treasures that include arms and armour, silver, paintings and furniture from the Order's time on the island of Malta, a fifteenth-century Flemish altar piece, and decorative jugs from the monks' pharmacy. After the dissolution of the monasteries, Henry VIII used the sixteenth-century

Priory precincts for storing army supplies, and under Elizabeth I, it housed the Revels Office, where thirty of Shakespeare's plays were registered. In the Gate's east tower, Hogarth's father ran a coffee house, and Edward Cave's *Gentleman's Magazine* was published with a young Dr Johnson writing the articles. In Victorian times, the St John Ambulance was founded here, inspired by the medical traditions of the Knights. People passing this very impressive gate daily are unaware of the wonderful treasures that are held there!

When we were working in Victoria I was sent to the Sun Electric Company in Charing Cross Road to obtain some silk flex. On leaving the premises with the flex, I crossed the road and decided to spend a few minutes in an amusement arcade on a pinball machine. I placed the flex on a machine at the side of me, and became engrossed in the play. At the end of the game, I looked around and found that the flex had been stolen. I went into the decline of a fourteen year old and cried and cried! Eventually I plucked up enough courage to return to Victoria, face the music and explain the loss. With the stars shining down on me, the people I was working for were sympathetic and I was let off the hook!

On one of the jobs in the West End, we were working quite close to Wardour Street. Each day I would pass by "Ley-Ons", one of the very few Chinese restaurants in London at that time. I could not pass without looking at the huge menu displayed in the window. All those lovely, exotic, oriental mouth-watering dishes that I was bursting to try and taste, but I could never afford to

178

dine there. I said to myself, "One day I shall eat here." And I did . . .

I began working with a Belgian electrician named Henri for long periods. He was a delightful man, and would take the trouble to explain everything in depth; not only electrical matters, but also worldly affairs, and especially romance, arousing my interests in so many subjects! London at this particular time had several continental butchers, which you do not see around today. They, of course, sold horse meat. We were still on rationing and meat was very scarce. Henri took me home one Saturday afternoon and introduced me to horsemeat. He cooked steaks for both of us; I thought they were delicious. I bought some from a continental butchers in Farringdon Road and took them home. My grandmother was as pleased as anything; not knowing that it was horsemeat! I informed Grandfather of the truth, thinking that he would readily accept it. How wrong I was! He went absolutely ballistic at the very thought of eating it. Consequently, I never brought any home ever again. Henri was having a love affair with the company secretary. Our boss greatly disapproved of this relationship, and of Henri, and showed his disdain whenever they were together. Eventually they were married. Henri would certainly have been sacked were it not for the fact that the secretary was so important to the company.

Very often I had to remain at our office in Clerkenwell Road. Close by was St Peter's Catholic Church where Gigli had sung, and opposite was Leather Lane and Hatton Garden. Facing us was

Lloyd's Tobacco Factory, so sweet-smelling pipe tobacco permeated the air all day long! Each morning I would leave home and catch the No. 555 Bloomsbury trolley bus to work. Sometimes, when I was a little short of money, I would walk. Close to where I worked was a "dining rooms", then numerous around London. The interiors all looked alike; dark-stained seating, partitioned by wood-panelled sections, accommodating four to six at a squeeze, with marble-topped tables. The menus were very basic, but offered good wholesome food. In the mornings smoked haddock, kippers, bacon and bubble (bubble and squeak), porridge, toast, dripping toast, large tea and small tea was available. At lunchtimes there would be steak and kidney puddings, steak and kidney pie, liver and bacon, and sausages and mash. The vegetables were all boiled; potatoes, cabbage and peas. Nothing was ever fried; chips in these establishments were unheard of. Sweets, the word "desserts" never in our vocabulary, were always suet pudding, treacle pudding, marmalade pudding and jam pudding, all served with custard. The proprietor, Ted Driscoll, forever-smiling Ted, employed me early in the mornings before I started work to toast the bread for him. I would sit in front of his coal fired range holding the bread in front of the fire with a toasting fork. For this I was given a large mug of tea and two slices of dripping toast. I was allowed to spread the dripping on my toast, which would have me going to the bottom of the dripping basin for the dark brown beef jelly, the tastiest part!

Catching the 555 trolley bus to work one morning with my sister, we were very near our destinations when the air raid warning sounded. She got off at her normal stop; I decided to alight from the bus before I reached Leather Lane. Getting off at Farringdon Road, I heard the familiar droning of a "doodlebug". Looking towards Smithfield Meat Market, directly in line with Farringdon Road, I could see a black V-1 that suddenly had cut its engine, and was gliding down towards me. Not knowing which way to turn, I stood in the doorway of a pub directly on the corner. It had huge plate glass windows which I never took any notice of at the time, as I was too focused on where the "doodlebug" was going to land. It hit the concrete building opposite to where I was standing, taking off the two top floors. Plumes of smoke soared high up into the sky, debris flew everywhere, and people were coming off the buses cut and bleeding from the glass. The glass from the pub next to where I had been standing had blown in — not out. My sister had run up Clerkenwell Road looking for me and was crying. She felt sure that I had been hit. On seeing me safe and sound, she turned around and headed back to her workplace, and I, in turn, carried on to mine. Amazingly, being so young, I don't think you have any sense of fear. I used to stand out with a neighbouring friend during raids, when shrapnel was flying around, and recall the unmistakable "ping" noise it made when metal hit metal. We would stand there looking up to the sky laughing! His mother would be screaming and yelling at us to come inside!

One of the first V-1's to hit London came down in Grove Road, Bethnal Green on 13 June 1944, killing six people, injuring thirty and making 200 homeless. On the final day of the V-1 and V-2 campaign, Tuesday 27 March 1945, at 7.21 a.m., V-2 hit Hughes Mansions in Vallance Road, Bethnal Green, where 134 residents lost their lives in a single stroke. That rocket was the 1,114[th] of the assault. A total of 2,550 V-1 and V-2's reached London between 12/13 June 1944 and 29 March 1945.

As a relief from the office in Clerkenwell, I was sent to Brimsdown to assist with the installation of an automatic telephone system. Brimsdown had a large cableworks company, spread over a very large area. It was pleasant, light work that suited me far better than threading conduit pipes and bending them at angles like I had to do at the factory in Holloway. Hammering holes into concrete by hand wasn't really my scene at all. The works had a large canteen that I rather liked going to, since they served chips with just about everything, and with spam and corned beef. In fact it was one of the few places that served chips at all. One lunchtime I could hear live music. Entering the vast hall that housed the canteen, I saw Big Bill Campbell and his Rocky Mountain Rhythm, with Peggy Bailey and his female vocalists "Sweetheart of the Golden West" on the stage. It was *Workers' Playtime*. This went out three times a week as a lunchtime road show, from factories and shop floors up and down the country. You would hear the announcement, "Workers' Playtime comes to you from somewhere in England." I found the whole thing quite entertaining, being amused by Big Bill passing round the applejack and moose meat sandwiches, when there was nothing to pass around! There was, of course, the other radio programme of *Music While You Work* that kept the war worker singing and humming through their working hours.

Occasionally, I would have to go through one of the factories making copper wire; white-hot metal stretching yards and yards, with banging and clanging as it passed through the huge rollers, and sparks flying everywhere. From that moment on I knew instinctively that I cared not for factories and foundries, or anything of an industrial nature, though circumstances then meant I did not have the choice.

Returning from Brimsdown one day to Clerkenwell, we were diverted. A V-2 Rocket had hit Smithfield Market killing over a hundred people. Smithfield Market's rooftops were all encased in glass, it was literally everywhere. With the "doodlebugs" you could hear them coming; with the V-2, there was never any time for sirens to be sounded, as they travelled faster than sound. The first experience of the V-2 was when I was walking home; it was close to midnight and I was just a few doors away, in total darkness, when suddenly a deafening noise shook the whole street from side to side and an enormous flash, almost like daylight, lit up the sky. A rocket had hit the other side of Bethnal Green Road, nearer Whitechapel. My first reaction was to fathom out what it could possibly be, since I had never heard an explosive noise like it before, and why was there no warning? Eventually information filtered through to enlighten us.

We were shortly to be diverted again, travelling up from Brimsdown to Liverpool Street Station when a "doodlebug" hit the railway line at Potters Bar. During these times you took everything in your stride and had to be philosophical, accepting whatever fate's hand was to deal you.

Still as young teenagers, come the weekends we would "go up West". My weekly wage of 15s would be approximately 75p in today's money. I would place my wage packet on the dinner table every Friday night, unopened, to present to my grandmother. 10s was taken for my keep, the remaining 5s was my pocket money to include fares and anything else.

We would take a bus to Tottenham Court Road, buy a packet of five Player's Weights cigarettes for the cinema and go to the Dominion in the 1s 9d seats. Coming out of the cinema, we would have a milkshake in the Black and White Milk Bar in Charing Cross Road. To us at that time it was really "living", though a dreadful drain on our pocket money to get through the rest of the week!

My sister had taken a position at the Bethnal Green Town Hall, and it was through her working there that she was able to trace our mother to Coventry. Through practically the whole of the war we did not know of her whereabouts. Communication was reestablished with her, and having no legitimate reasons or excuses for her absence, she returned to London for the day to see us. It was an odd feeling, seeing her again. I felt no anger at

184

what she had done, I was just happy to see her. If anyone was a good actress, she was. The years of irresponsible motherhood were swept under the carpet, the subject of her behaviour never raised, never questioned. She came home to No. 74 like nothing had ever occurred; our grandparents behaved in the same manner. Not one word of reprimand for deserting her children was uttered. My own belief is that she must have given our grandmother some money, and that made everything fine.

On 7 May 1945, Germany surrendered. VE Day was declared on 8 May 1945. With some of the boys in our street, we decided to "go up West." If ever one experienced a city going completely wild, this was it! GI's were hanging out of windows at Rainbow Corner, people had clambered up lampposts, dancing, singing everywhere, smiling, laughing, crying and shouting. The crowds were 4ft deep. Piccadilly, Leicester Square, Coventry Street, Regent Street, Oxford Street, and Trafalgar Square were all just a huge conglomerated mass of people, rejoicing that the war was finally over! Huge crowds had gathered outside Buckingham Palace, many dressed in red, white and blue. The King, Queen and the Princesses came out on the balcony and waved to the crowd.

In Piccadilly Circus I began to feel quite sick and started to vomit. It took over an hour to get out of the crowds and get a bus home. I told my grandmother that I didn't feel well and she immediately came to the conclusion that I had been drinking. The following day she realised that I was genuinely ill, and accompanied

185

me to the doctor. Doctor Rockfeldt in Hackney Road diagnosed a grumbling appendix. The doctor informed me that I would probably have to have it removed the following year. How wrong his diagnosis was! I got peritonitis twenty-five years later! Grandmother saw to it that I did not go sick; there was never any sympathy in that area. I went to work, doubled-up in pain and came home from work still suffering. Her remedy was always to go to bed when you came home.

It took me a long time to realise that I was not really cut out for the job I was doing. At that young age, I still did not know what I really wanted to do. Having no one with whom I could rationally discuss where my talents lay and what I would be better at doing, I soldiered on. It didn't matter what you did in our grandmother's eyes, so long as you worked. One day I suddenly decided to take a sabbatical and visit my mother in Coventry. I found her living with another man, whom, from day one, I did not like. I didn't like his looks, his manner or, anything else about him. I was deeply hurt that my mother was living with him. Having been brought up in an environment where morals, ethics, and codes of conduct were high especially if you were married, unmarried couples who were living together were considered as something alien and shameful. I carried this sense of shame within me for a long, long time. Apart from my sister, who felt the same way about our mother's choice, we never mentioned it to anyone. We were perhaps sitting in judgement, comparing him to our father, but as far as we were concerned there was no contest. He didn't have our father's intelligence, manners or breeding. Our mother recognised our feelings but ignored them, and tried to engineer a way for us to accept him.

Arriving back from Coventry, I found a job in a distribution warehouse in Cambridge Heath Road It was a little more interesting than the electrical work. Most of the employees there had returned from the services, unmistakable by their "demob" suits, raincoats and hats. It was hard for them to re-adapt to civilian life and work in a warehouse after being to far-flung places. For me, it was interesting to hear their stories of naval engagements, desert battles and the theatres of war they had been involved in. The managing director came to me one day, and told me he would like me to work in the office. He asked to see my grandmother to discuss my prospects, so a meeting took place and I was promoted into the office. I was given lessons in typing and general office procedure; I learnt by heart the prices and tax on every item we sold. I used to take sandwiches that my grandmother made, which were of doorstop magnitude! When it came to lunchtime I was too embarrassed to put them on top of the desk, so instead I would break a piece off in the desk drawer, and place the food piece by piece into my mouth. If I could afford it, I would buy a tongue sandwich from Lou Napolitano's on the corner; they made fabulous ones, the bread was so fresh, with real butter and the tongue melted in your mouth. Grandmother could never match it.

Later on, I was given the task of making out all the invoices for clients. This was to prove a grave mistake; I was left solely on my own to execute the invoices on a portable typewriter. What should have been a "call over", a checking over of the items with another person, was never carried out. It was never even suggested. I don't think they realised that an accuracy check should have taken place. This resulted in errors being made and customers complaining. I was sent back to the warehouse.

Mother was later to return to London with her beau. It was hurtful to us that after she obtained a flat, there was never any mention of her providing a home for us. Her boyfriend took first place, while we carried on living with our grandparents at No. 74. We could only describe it as selfish, insensitive behaviour.

Some of the boys down the street and I decided to join the ATC (Air Training Corps). There was No.416 Squadron in Bethnal Green Road where we duly enrolled. It was great fun, learning Morse code, tapping away on the Morse keyboard, sending each other rude messages! The greatest thing of all was flying. On several weekends we would go to Wethersfield in Essex. I was very small for my age, so the parachute pack practically covered me! We would fly in Avro Ansons or Airspeed Oxfords, both of them training craft. Some pilots were not too happy as they were unable to have weekend leave, having to stay behind at the airfield to take cadet brats into the air. Some pilots would try to frighten us by doing all kinds of manoeuvres, but the more dives and circles in the sky they made, the better I liked it! The cabins were not pressurized, and you could feel your head being pressed down, a most unusual sensation. We had to keep a log book of the flights and of the altitude climbed. We spent a week away in Felixstowe on Sunderland aircraft, draining out the floats and general aircraft maintenance. I was as happy as a sandboy, being involved on those Sunderlands, and was very sad when that week came to an end. The ATC would occasionally hold a dance on a Saturday night, my first introduction to dancing, which I discovered I liked. Our hall was behind the Post Office in Bethnal Green Road. One thing that sticks out in my memory was the mirrored globe on the ceiling, turning when the lights were dimmed, and multi-coloured rays bouncing off that glittering ball to the tune of "Goodnight Sweetheart" at the closing of the evening's dance. I think the tune of "Goodnight Sweetheart" was the finale to nearly every dance.

On one occasion I popped into my grandfather's "new" local, the Shakespeare next to Bethnal Green Police Station. We had given the pub the name of "The Shake". He was there with his cronies drinking, his favourite beverage "mild and bitter" straight from the barrel. In those days flying was not a way of life as it is today; with the exception of RAF personnel, very few then had the opportunity to fly. For grandfather and his friends, flying was something they had only read about. He would proudly have me tell his friends of my endeavors, the altitude I had flown at, about the aircraft I had flown in, and the aerodromes I had visited. His friends would nod and look up in awe. Grandfather would repeat some of the questions I had already been asked. "How many thousand feet did you fly at?" he would say, he just liked to hear it! If you remained, it would invariably turn into a few songs being sung, mostly Irish. It was hard to convince my grandfather that most of these Irish songs that brought tears to the eyes were written mainly in Tin Pan Alley, New York by some Jewish composers.

Being so close to "the nick", the police used to drive black Wolseley cars to the back of the station into a yard. The yard also accommodated horses used by the mounted police. What fascinated me about these cars was the illuminated Wolseley sign on the radiator. You could spot a police car a mile off, by the light of the logo. There were stories about this particular police station, which once had a detective by the name of "Nutty Sharpe". He got the name "Nutty" from the angle he wore his bowler hat. It was alleged that he arrested the whole of the "Whizz Mob", a pickpocket organisation operating at a racecourse, put them all on a double-decker bus and drove the bus all the way back to the Bethnal Green station! In the winter evenings, just outside the police station, was "Potato Jack's", his barrow containing glowing coals and large potatoes stuck on spikes, ready to serve to the customer. Jack would remove a potato from the spikes, and serve it to you doused in vinegar, peppered and salted, and placed in newspaper. Off you would go, warming your hands on the large pebble-shaped tuber, enjoying every mouthful as you walked down Bethnal Green Road!

Along with our aunts, we would continue to go to the local cinemas. At this time on the radio, Charlie Chester had a show called *Stand Easy*. There was a character called "Whippet Quick". My Aunt May with her daughter Sheila went to the Excelsior. During the performance they observed a man masturbating a few seats away from them. Aunt May dubbed him "Whippet Quick" thereafter, and whenever any one of us went to the cinema, we would be asked if "Whippet Quick" was there!

Aunt Winnie, the youngest of grandmother's daughters, was more like a sister; she was eight years older than us. At night, when Winnie and my sister went upstairs to bed, I would hide in the darkness of the recess of my bedroom door. As they passed with a solitary candle, I would make noises to frighten them. It got to a stage where my sister was too frightened to go to bed! They would yell down to my grandmother to get me to stop it. My grandmother would shout up at me to behave, but could never refrain from laughing when doing so.

Winnie held a clerical position for a firm which owned a chain of butchers; it meant her staying at home less and less. Eventually, it came to light that she was romancing her boss, who was already married. A chauffer-driven Armstrong Siddeley would arrive outside our house to collect her, and on the odd occasion her boss would come in. Out of all the family, Winnie was the only one who married into wealth.

Returning from work one evening, I caught a No. 8 bus at the corner of Shoreditch High Street and Bethnal Green Road. There was no room at the bottom of the bus, so I ascended to the top. I was met by a thick curtain of cigarette smoke that you could cut with

191

a knife. Looking around for a seat, I found my grandfather sitting there. He was returning from the docks. I sat beside him, and everyone upstairs in that bus must have been smoking. A man sitting at the front of the bus was having a coughing spasm; it sounded awful, but my grandfather, much to my horror shouted out "Die, you bastard, die!." I wanted to fold up and die with embarrassment!

There was a saying we used to quote in such circumstances:

> It ain't the cough that carries you off
> It's the coffin they carry you off in.

One of the few music halls still remaining is The Hackney Empire. It was another form of live entertainment that we cared for. The "'Ackney Empire" was built in 1901 and, thank God, it is still going strong. It was here that some of the old time greats trod the boards: Charlie Chaplin, Stan Laurel, and Marie Lloyd. We also saw Max Miller, Arthur Askey, Cavan O'Connor, Leo Fould, Maxie Bacon, Cyril Fletcher, Derek Roy, Phyllis Dixie and Jane of the *Daily Mirror*. I can also recall Peter Sellers when he was third on the bill. Later, Ted Heath and his band, accompanied by vocalists Lita Rosa and Dickie Valentine, appeared. We were mad about the "big band sound".

On 8 June 1946 our ATC Squadron was invited to the victory parade. We assembled at St Paul's Cathedral with other ATC squadrons and marched from the cathedral through Admiralty Arch and down The Mall to the Victoria Memorial, immediately in front of Buckingham Palace. We sat on the lower steps of the memorial and watched the finest military parade from the four corners of the earth. The King and Queen, together with the Princesses Elizabeth and Margaret, drove past in an open landau, so close that you could almost reach out and touch them. They looked absolutely magnificent! Military bands, U.S. Marines and GI's, Arab legions, contingents from New Zealand, Australia, South Africa, India and the Commonwealth, regiment after regiment, then the British Army, tanks and armoured cars paraded before us. There was a Royal Air Force fly-past. Wartime celebrities such as Winston Churchill, Lord Mountbatten, Field Marshalls Alexander and Montgomery, Generals Dwight Eisenhower, Mark Clarke, Charles de Gaulle and Emperor Haile Selassie all passed by, so near to where we were sitting. We had one of the finest views of the whole parade. It seemed endless; it went on and on. This must have been about the most magnificent display of all times. I doubt very much if we will ever see the like of it again.

Close to our ATC Headquarters in Bethnal Green Road, a bomb site had been turned into a fairground. There was a boxing marquee which used to be quite popular with the locals. You were invited to put on the gloves and go three rounds with one of the fairground's appointed pugilists for a fiver. Bethnal Green has been the birthplace of many well-known boxers; practically everyone had, at one time, boxed, either at school or at one of the boxing clubs that existed in the East End. It

193

was therefore no surprise that the fair had many takers willing to get into the ring.

We were quite enthusiastic at following the amateur boxers, and would see boxing matches at the York Hall, Hoxton Baths and Shoreditch Town Hall. We had the boxing clubs at the Oxford House in Mape Street, The Repton in Victoria Park Square and at Eton Manor. Several of the boys from these clubs became professional. Two of our favourites were Joe Lucy and Sammy McCarthy; they had style and craftsmanship, and you were guaranteed a good performance from both of those boys.

At about this time I joined the Mansford Youth Club, which was for the sixteen and seventeen year olds, although much older girls and boys attended. It was held in a converted two-storey garage; the ground floor had wooden parquet flooring, ideal for dancing, and a stage. Upstairs were billiard and table-tennis tables, and a small bar that served tea and biscuits. It was here that I learned to dance, and for the next six years dancing became a non-stop pursuit. This was the age of the big bands. Glenn Miller, Artie Shaw, Count Basie, Tommy Dorsey, and Lionel Hampton; and the age of great singers such as Frank Sinatra, Perry Como, Billy Eckstein, Ella Fitzgerald, Jo Stafford and a host of others.

It was here that I came into regular contact with Reggie and Ronnie Kray, who were also members. We never dreamed that in later years they would receive such notoriety. When they were about ten years of age they would come to St Peter's Avenue to visit their friend from Daniel Street School, Patsy Beauvoir, who lived opposite St Peter's Church. Patsy had the making, even then, of a tear-away, and grew up to become a genuine one. Patsy's father, a short wizened man who looked much older than his years, was plagued by ill health, his weakened body bent over, a cigarette permanently dangling from his mouth, coughing his heart out, never realizing that his smoking was killing him. His mother was tall and slim. She made a radical "Eliza Doolittle" change from being a plain and drab female to an overnight glamour girl when the American GI's came over. At weekends, she would put her make up on, get herself "dolled" up and "go up West" in pursuit of pleasure. For her, and many others like her, living in the East End was a hum-drum existence, and it was not difficult to understand that they needed a stimulus of colour and excitement in their lives, to compensate for the grey drabness of their environment.

On one occasion when the twins came to see Patsy, my cousin Sheila was playing with the vicar's daughter in St Peter's Churchyard. Reggie and Ronnie came over from Patsy's house and tied cousin Sheila's long blonde plaits to a tree. They got up to boyish, mischievous pranks just like the rest of us. They lived in Vallance Road, the other side of Bethnal Green Road. We regularly saw them with their brother Charlie at Pelicci's café, which we all frequented. Uncle Alf used to drink with Charlie, their father, in the Marquis of Cornwallis. Several years later when I was catching the No. 8 bus in Bethnal Green Road, Reggie Kray was standing at the same bus stop; we both got on and sat together upstairs — Reggie paid the bus fares. Even at that time, I had no knowledge of their infamy. He was quietly spoken, just as I had always known him to be, and we chatted casually all the way to the West End. I got off at Tottenham Court Road and Reggie remained on the bus. I never saw either of the twins again. It later became known to me that they were accompanying George Raft, Judy Garland and many other celebrities whilst running "The Firm" (The Krays' organisation). I was absolutely astounded when I read articles about them in the newspapers.

This was an age when we were "jive" mad, the drape suit, "guards-back" overcoats and Stetson hats were the height of fashion in the East End. I was not yet in the money league to afford the type of clothing I would have liked. I bought a blue serge suit from Billy Saunders in Wellington Row, but whilst giving it a good pressing from the iron heated on the gas stove for a dance that evening, I badly scorched the trouser turn up. With ingenuity, I cut a piece of cloth from behind the jacket lapel and glued it to the burnt part of the turn up! That night, I stood well back in the dance hall, in case anyone should spot my handiwork, dancing only when the lights were dimmed!

We would dance at the Mansford two to three times a week; you would see the same following of people. Tubby Hutchinson would come into the club wearing a white riding belted raincoat and a grey Stetson that he never removed, even when he was "jiving". No one ever dared to tell Tubby how ridiculous he looked, jiving in them! Storky Walker, with his frizzy hair and horn-rimmed glasses, was a great jiver, dancing very erect with the most serious of expressions. You would hardly ever see Storky smile when he was on the floor! Tony Martin was also a terrific dancer, great with the girls too! Stocky in build, blue eyes and dark wavy hair, with a charming smile! Dumpsy Davis, whose brother Jimmy was a professional middleweight, would come up behind you if you were not watching, clench a fist and place it on your head, and with his other fist hit it like a hammer! I am apt to believe he got this from watching the "Three Stooges" too often. It was not very pleasant if you were on the receiving end, but everyone accepted that nothing would ever change him! It was here at the Mansford that I learned to fox trot, quickstep, rumba and tango. The club introduced us to opera, and I saw my first major opera "La Boheme", at Sadlers Wells, followed by several others at this theatre. These experiences broadened my horizons in music, firmly establishing me as a fan for life.

The club would also arrange weekends under canvas alongside the river close to Runnymede. We had some wonderful times there! Someone once brought a portable gramophone player, one of those old wind-up handle types; the record selection was very limited and the same ones were played over and over again which drove you to distraction! One I recall that virtually seared my brain was "*I met Sally Pringle when she was single, dat, dat, data, dat dow sir*". Each time I heard that record played I felt like jumping in the river.

Wanting to look as smart as several of the other boys and feeling a little bit out of it, I wore my grandmother

197

down enough to persuade her to take a loan on my behalf, so that I could have a tailor made "drape suit". When she asked me how much the suit was, and I told her £25, she absolutely went into orbit! However, she arranged a loan with Mrs Andrews across the street. Having got my way, I went to Levine's in Green Street, now Roman Road and ordered a mid-blue pinhead suit. The suit, when I put it on for the very first time, elevated me! I thought I looked the cat's whiskers and could now join the others with confidence.

"Barry's" was now my first opportunity to wear my new drape suit, as it was a dance hall above Burton's the Tailors in the Narrow Way, Hackney. It was run by Barry Langruish. Barry was softly spoken, tall, elegant, and refined with dyed-blond wavy hair. He had two sisters, Doris and Winnie, whose hair was as black as Barry's was blonde, and as Barry was handsome, they looked as though they were the unfortunate ones related to Cinderella! For the boys who attended Barry's, the trademark was to wear white socks. If you were walking down the street and you were seen wearing white socks, you would get a shout of "Barry Boy". Barry never had live music, only records. It was more like a club than a dance hall; here you got to know everyone. The girls would be sitting, the boys would be standing. To approach a girl to dance, you would just say "Coming round?". To say "Would you like to dance?" was not in our vocabulary! In those days, I must have taken many girls home, but I must say they were never promiscuous. It was mainly a smooch; we called it a "lumber". At Barry's, two brothers from Bethnal Green used to attend, George and Lenny Walker. George was of medium height, with straight, lank blonde hair, while Lenny was short, dark-haired and like a tiger if upset. George would talk in a flat monotone voice; there were no highs, or lows, or heights in his conversation — it was devoid of expression! Whenever I said to George "How are you?" he would reply, "How am I? . . . 'umping those fucking 'taters up and down those cobbles, 'aint worth a carrot!." George, of course, worked as a porter in Covent Garden, so he was telling me that, "Wheeling a heavy load of potatoes in a wheelbarrow over the cobbled streets of Covent Garden just wasn't worth it!." George later became a taxi driver. At Barry's he always seemed to know which girl I had taken home. On one occasion, I took a girl back to her home in Walthamstow; the following day, dear George, always inquisitive, wanted to know how I got on. I was always non-committal in such matters. I simply replied, "Nothing." George found this very hard to accept. "Listen," he said, "you don't go all the way to Walthamstow for nothing!" George never ever believed me; the truth was that apart from a smooch, nothing did happen! Lenny, his brother, was as small as he was, and as tough as they come. One evening at Barry's, he got involved in a dispute with some boys from Bermondsey who were twice his size. They went down into a little courtyard at the side of The Mermaid Pub for a "straightener". A "straightener" was a term that was used to "fight it out". Lenny put the three Bermondsey boys down, left them lying in the courtyard and came back to the dance completely unperturbed!

In the "Barry" dancing years, I befriended three boys from Goldsmith Row: Albert Styman whose mother owned a pub, the Star of the East, Franie Evans, whose parents were proprietors of a dining rooms; and Terry Saunders, who was in the Merchant Navy. Albert was a beautifully sophisticated pianist who trained under Sidney Bright, Geraldo the bandleader's brother. He would often play at the pub and was always welcomed at parties. One Sunday morning, we were having a drink listening to Albert playing a medley of some fine tunes, such as "Laura", "Smoke gets in your eyes", "Nancy" and many others. He was approached by one of the patrons we called "Smiffy". Smiffy always wore a black cheese cutter cap, a black suit and shirt with no collar, and the lapels of his jacket were always smothered in fag ash! Albert was in the middle of playing "Laura" in his very stylish way. Smiffy, leaning up against the piano, extended his arm with a pint glass of beer across the top of the piano and said to Albert "'ere Albert, 'ow abaht playing 'Who's sorry now'?" In that one moment Smiffy destroyed the aura of the sophisticated music.

A few doors away from the Star of the East was a greengrocers, which Albert and some of the other boys knew as "Fat Alice's". Alice, the wife of the proprietor, was indeed a woman of large proportion with a nice pleasant face. Unbeknown to me, they would pay a visit to Alice when the husband wasn't there, and she would give them "a levy and frank", Cockney rhyme for masturbation.

Franie was the shortest one of us, and of stocky build; he would call at my home early on Saturday evenings to find out what I was going to wear that night. His father would stand outside their dining rooms with a snow-white starched apron worn very high, while his mother worked like a Trojan inside. He would disappear down to the Cat & Mutton pub at the end of the Broadway leaving Mrs Evans to do just about everything. Franie was a porter in Convent Garden who, like several of the others in Covent Garden and Spitalfields, became a taxi driver.

Terry remained in the Merchant Navy until coming ashore to get married, knowing full well that he would be called up if he stepped down the gangway before he had reached the age of twenty-six. As expected, he spent his National Service in the Military Police. It was through this man's influence that my life turned around and he pointed me in the right direction.

Our dancing tentacles would reach out to the Royal in Tottenham in mid-week, the Lyceum in the Strand on Sunday nights, and the York Hall or Shoreditch Town Hall on most Saturdays. At the Royal we would dance to the Ray Ellington Quartet. At the Lyceum, it was the Oscar Rabin Band, and sometimes Vic Lewis at the Shoreditch Town Hall. The band leaders and the vocalists got to know us quite well because of our regular attendance. Outside the Lyceum was a coffee stall, no longer seen around London. We would have a coffee and a sausage sandwich, then start walking home. It was nothing for us to walk home from the Strand all the way back to Bethnal Green.

On Saturdays, in order to supplement my income, I got a job with a friend selling salt and vinegar from a horse and cart around Highbury. We would buy a gallon of ascetic acid and a large tin of caramel from a shop at the corner of Weymouth Terrace and Hackney Road. We would then ride to the end of Hoxton Market, where there was a stone horse trough. We used to place a wooden barrel with the acid and caramel under the water tap and fill it up, giving it a good stir, and "presto" — vinegar. The salt would be in block form that we would saw off, as required. We would go knocking at doors around Highbury shouting, "Salt and vinegar, salt and vinegar." Housewives would come out with their jugs for us to fill up, and saw off a piece of salt from the block. We would have a slap-up meal at lunchtime and buy ourselves a packet of Royalty cigarettes. The Saturday income was nearly as much as I earned all week. I look back now and think, "However did I do that?" going through those streets shouting "Salt and vinegar", but then I realised that the driving force was to earn more money, so embarrassment went out of the window.

Hoxton was considered rough, even by Bethnal Green standards. Nile Street, or "the Nile," as it was known, had a terrible reputation in my younger years; people were afraid to walk down it. So many stories abounded, that if you entered the Nile the chance of being robbed, beaten up or having your throat cut was more than likely to happen. Our father often referred to the "Jago", that was another place that brought fear and trepidation, even to East Enders, at the mere mention of the name. I never found out until later years where in Hoxton it actually was. It was, in fact, the Old Nichol Rookery, one of London's worst slums. A Reverend Osbourne Jay of the Holy Trinity persuaded the author Arthur Morrison to visit the area, resulting in a book being written by him, titled A *Child of the Jago*. This was a fictionalised account of the life of a child in the slum conditions in the Old Nichol, renaming the Old Nichol as "The Jago". The name Jago stuck, and the area was known as this thereafter. In 1886 practically 6,000 people were packed into this area. The mortality rate was twice that of Bethnal Green, and four times that of London as a whole. One in four children died before they reached one year of age. In 1844, the concentration was eight people to a small house, and there were 1,400 houses in an area less than 400 yards long. John Hollingshead, of the *Morning Post*, wrote *Ragged London* in 1861, and noted that the Jago had grown even more neglected in the last twenty years as old houses decayed and bona-fide trades became a cover up for thieves and prostitutes. *The Builder* in 1863 noted the numbers living in unfit basement cellars, the lack of sanitation, and that fresh running water was only available for ten to twelve minutes each day, excepting Sundays.

Society demanded a change for the clearance of the Old Nichol Street Rookery; which resulted in a forceful demonstration led by the Reverend Osbourne Jay. Charles Booth had already seen at first hand and noted the extreme poverty. Demolition actually began before Arthur Morrison's book was published. The campaign was such a success that the Prince of Wales officially opened the new estate in 1900, saying, "Few indeed will forget this site, who had read Mr Morrison's *A Child of the Jago.*"

While new flats replaced the existing slums, many still lived in appalling conditions. The original inhabitants were moved, creating new overcrowding and more slums, in Dalston and Bethnal Green. At this time assistance was unavailable for the displaced, and this only added to the suffering and misery of the slums' former residents.

During the 1930s the reputation of Hoxton and its infamous areas remained, and we would only venture into the area during the daylight, most certainly not in darkness. Hoxton has now become the "in" place to be, with its smart restaurants and celebrity residents. Yet even now, I would still not walk around there in the wee small hours.

In 1947 I realised that it would not be too long before I was called up for National Service. To fill out the time, I got a job at Wren's Shaped Ply Veneers in Fuller Street. The money was good, but oh so boring! I literally stood at a machine all day long drilling holes into squares of shaped veneered ply; while I was drilling I was daydreaming. One day, I was daydreaming so intently that the drill went straight through my left hand index finger. I pulled my finger away and tore it in two. Off I went under escort to the Mildmay Mission Hospital for treatment, having my arm in a sling for two months or more. In this factory one of the staff was deaf and dumb, known to every one as "Dummy". At home one day whilst grandmother was sitting there, the telephone rang. I answered the call, and after a brief conversation put the telephone receiver down. Grandmother asked me who had called. I replied, "Dummy from work." She sat there for a full five minutes before the penny dropped. "You silly daft sod, how could Dummy ring you?" Such was my sense of humour! On another occasion she was telling me about her wedding at the Red Church in Bethnal Green Road. I said to her, "Didn't we have a lovely time?" Once again with some delay she replied, "How did you know, you weren't there!"

A film came out in 1947, *It always rains on Sunday* with John McCallum and Googie Withers. It depicted Bethnal Green. Many Bethnal Green residents protested at being portrayed as crooks, "chancers" and murderers. The Cinematograph Exhibitors Association's reviewer declared it "an unsavoury film . . . with an appeal only to the broad minded". One particular line in the film by Googie Withers was, "I wish there was no place like Bethnal Green." Some thirty-odd years later I was with this lovely couple on board a ship. I brought the subject up with Miss Withers of the line she used, and we laughed about it! John McCallum, who is an Australian, told me that to get the East End accent right for the film, he went to Eddie Phillips, the boxer, who had a pub, the Rising Sun, in Globe Road, Bethnal Green.

Parties in the East End for our age group were a regular feature, and were very well conducted; I cannot recall any incident where there was any disruption. Records had taken over from the piano, though if one still had a piano and someone who could play, so much the better. The "Knees up Mother Brown" era had gone. One party I attended in Stepney reminded me of a Laurel and Hardy scene! A bungalow bath was turned upside down, resting on the backs of two chairs, with a table cloth placed over it, and this served as a bar. It goes to show how innovative people were!

Clothing became the number one item in our lives, it was suits, suits, suits. The boys would have tailor-made drape suits, the girls tailor-made drape costumes. The material had to be bird's eye, pinhead, diagonal, hopsack or barathea. The back of the suit could only be seamless, wide shouldered and single breasted. Our tailors were Levine's in Green Street and Hoxton, Solomon's & Temples in Hackney Road, and Alfred Myers in Old Street.

When entering a dance hall, several of the boys would walk with the right arm held straight down the side, hand held part open, with the fingers curled as though the whole limb was paralysed. One of the boys had a suit with shoulder padding which was too wide for his shoulders, so he would keep bouncing his shoulders up and down to prevent his jacket slipping off. It was almost as though he had a nervous affliction! Our shirts had cut-away collars, spear point collars, and spread collars. Most of us wore Stetson hats, worn squarely on the head. We were influenced a very great

206

deal by Hollywood gangster and tough guy films in the way we dressed.

Haircuts were also of great importance to us. We would go to Dave's in Hackney Road for a "DA" (Duck's Arse), a Tony Curtis hairstyle, having a singe, or a Prashana hair friction. Prashana was a heavily scented hair lotion that we thought was wonderful. Looking back, it smelt like something out of a Turkish brothel. Sometimes, I would rub my hair vigorously with a towel in front of the fire until I made it frizzy. I thought that I had developed a new hairstyle!

Most of us would gather outside Pellicci's Café in Bethnal Green Road; the Pelliccis have been there as long as I can remember, and the interior of the café has remained exactly the same, even after all these years. Their parents hailed from Lucca in Tuscany; many years ago they settled in the East End and opened the café in 1900. They had two cafés in my teenage years, the original, that is still there facing the Red Church, and the other was on the corner of Mape Street. The Pellicci brothers were all nice boys; Terry, Jeep, Pete and Nev. Jeep, whose name was Elio, was given this unusual nickname by his brothers; it derives from Popeye's son in the cartoons. Today Nev, as we know him, his real name is Nevio, is the only surviving brother, and with his daughter and son Nevio junior. He continues to run the business. Pellicci's has become quite famous and is frequented by many film celebrities. In fact the Pelliccis have attained a cult status. Rarely can you enter the establishment to find a table on any day of the week. The interior has remained the same for years with its wood-panelled Art Deco marquetry, and vivid yellow vitrolite paneling of the counter making it both unique and interesting.

Characters abounded in Bethnal Green, particularly around Pellicci's. A permanent fixture was Freddie Burrows, who worked in Spitalfields market as a porter. We gave him the name of "Ruckie Boy". He loved to use the word "rucking" (a telling off) in his vocabulary. "I gave him a rucking", "I gave her a rucking" . . . just about everyone got a rucking from Freddie at one time or another. Dear old Freddie, with his cheese cutter worn flat on his head and knotted scarf, had an affinity with cart horses and behaved in a manner that made him appear twenty years older than his years. Another character was "Arthur the Suss". Arthur looked more like a villain than a villain, which he never was. But unfortunately for him, he was always being picked up by the police on suspicion of some crime or another, hence he became known around "the Green" as "Arthur the Suss". We had "Trini", whose Christian name was Patsy! He acquired the nickname from a song by Trini Lopez, "If I had a hammer", as he would use a hammer to smash a shop window for an article, specifically ordered by one of his clients. We all knew Harry Herbert who was lithe and slim, and a boxer at one time, although his walk was strangely feminine! Those who didn't know him, and might have thought otherwise, would have made a grave misjudgement! On one occasion we lined up at the cooked meat shop in Bethnal Green Road, for meat for his greyhound; we stood in the long queue that took ages, and by the time he got home the greyhound was dead! Then there were the Smith brothers, the Treseden brothers, and Charlie Bins. Charlie got his name from the glasses he wore. Glasses were always referred to as bins. He passed a remark to Ronnie Kray on one occasion asking him about his wife, namely referring to his homosexuality. Charlie knew something that I was completely unaware of — consequently it was to have repercussions. Charlie was paid a visit and worked over. The Brown twins, George and Jimmy, and Teddy and Checker Berry were all colourful personalities, and very often, the Kray twins, and their brother Charlie, would congregate outside Pellicci's café. Bethnal Green was referred to as "the Green", the locality "the Manor". A good-looking girl was known as "a brahma" and a prostitute was known as "a brass", not that we had any dealings with the latter! The girls would arrive with their hair in curlers, hidden by a turban, and wearing no make up as meeting altogether like this led to finding out where everyone was going that evening!

On Sunday mornings if it was dry, we would take a walk through to the flower market in Columbia Road, just two streets away from where we lived. We walked on through to Brick Lane, then Petticoat Lane into Bell Lane. Close by was a record stall, where we would stand and listen to all the latest record releases. This was our regular Sunday morning rendezvous, meeting up with some of the boys and chatting about the previous night's events.

We acquired a second-hand record player from a radio shop next to the Red Church in Bethnal Green road. I would buy a record of my choice one week, and my sister the next. Quite naturally, the type of music we chose was not of our grandparent's taste. Now and then, to arouse their interest, we would buy a record that they would like. We purchased "The Laughing Policeman"; it was bought for a particular reason so that if either grandparent was in a grumpy mood, I could play it. Before long, one of them would start laughing, then the other who would find it difficult to keep a straight face! It was a great way of breaking the ice and maintaining a more harmonious atmosphere in the home! One of the other records was called "The Box". It started off with:

> As I was walking on the beach one day,
> Much to my surprise,
> When I discovered (at this point),
> A boomp, boomp; (noise),
> Right before my eyes . . .

This drove my grandmother absolutely spare; she wanted to know what was in the box, which of course the song never revealed. It gave us a great kick seeing her trying to fathom out what it was. If we happened to have any records of an Irish nature, we would play them to see our grandfather "turn the taps on" at the drop of a hat!

As we were nearly eighteen and on the verge of being called up for National Service, we started to visit the pubs, both in Hackney and Bethnal Green. In those days, they had more or less taken over the music halls.

We would only go to those where there was entertainment! They would have an MC, most of them gay, and they certainly made those places popular; they sang, told jokes and were excellent in returning any wisecracks made with the rapidity of a machine gun! Many of the patrons would go up on stage with just the accompaniment of a piano, and render a song or two. Some were quite talented, others were not. Nevertheless it was usually a good Saturday night out. If one particular pub was not "humming", we would visit another. We had the Green Gate in Bethnal Green Road, the Basin House in Kingsland High Street, the Nelson in Morning Lane, Hackney and the Dew Dragon in Homerton. We never drank to excess, mainly brown ales, graduating to light ales, rarely drinking spirits of any description. If we were dancing at Barry's we would use a small pub next door, the Mermaid, for the interval between dancing. Little did I know at the time but this pub was to play a very significant part in my life.

Saturday night was when we really dressed "up to the nines"! Great care and attention was paid to how we looked before we set foot out onto the street. Apart from the women, the men were always eyeing each other up to see how each other dressed, or if anyone was wearing a new suit. The drape suit, the Stetson hat placed dead centre, rarely worn at an angle, was adopted from the film *The Killers* with Burt Lancaster who had a great influence on us at that time in what we wore, and even the facial expressions of trying to look hard and serious! If only I had known then that I would be in the company of Burt Lancaster in later years, sailing from Thailand to Australia, I would have never had thought this possible! One guy, who I thought really looked more menacing than any other, was Bobby Ramsey. He was a boxer, a real tough hombre, who looked every inch a gangster, although of course he wasn't. In the winter, the guards back overcoats, in either grey or navy, together with a silk paisley scarf, would be worn. If ever you stood in the Green Gate in Bethnal Green Road on a Saturday night, you would think you were in the company of gangsters and hoodlums. It was like a scene out of a movie in Chicago! Appearances, however, can be very deceptive; most were all gainfully employed.

If we were at Barry's at the closing of a dance and we were not taking a girl home, we would make for "Smithy's" next to the bus garage, just off of London Fields for steak and chips. At other times we would go to a restaurant in Bethnal Green Road on the corner of Mansford Street.

There was this wonderful story of one of the boys whose relative dropped dead with a heart attack in Southend. The family could not afford for the services of an undertaker to bring him back to London, so they arranged to have the body brought back in a friend's van. Picking up the corpse in Southend they stopped off for a cup of tea on the way back. When they vacated the roadside café they discovered to their horror that the van had been stolen. The van and the corpse were never recovered to this day.

In summertime, we would make for Larkswood in Chingford. Larkswood was an open air lido swimming pool. Several of the boys took up weight-lifting, developing their bodies in an attempt to resemble Charles Atlas, strutting around the pool being admired by the girls. One character very well-known at this time was a fellow called Arthur Mason. Arthur had a beautiful physique, quite tanned and used to wear white trunks, so he stood out more than anyone in Larkswood! We would often see him at the Royal in Tottenham, with a blonde actress, Vera Day. Arthur was always very pleasant to talk to. We were most surprised when we went to see *Mr Roberts* at the Coliseum starring Tyrone Power. Arthur was in the cast playing a US sailor!

During this period, all the big names were coming over from America. The London Casino in Soho and the London Palladium were the Mecca for all these Hollywood stars. Father took my sister to see the Ink Spots — he was a very great fan and I was quite irked at not being asked.

One hot summer's evening we had a milkshake and other edibles I should never have eaten, at the Black and White Milk Bar in Charing Cross Road. We managed to get tickets to a performance at the London Casino where Sophie Tucker was appearing. We were seated up in "the God's", the seats practically touching the theatre ceiling; you couldn't get any higher. The whole theatre was sweltering under the heat — air conditioned theatres were never heard of, and I think, even to this day, there are still many that are without it.

I began to feel quite nauseous, but determined not to miss the star of the show, I held out as long as I could, before I made a mad dash to the fire exit stairs and was as sick as a dog!

Seeing the film *Up in Arms* starring Danny Kaye, I became an instant fan. His sophisticated style as a comedian was quite different to anything I had ever seen. When it became known that he was coming to London, I was determined to get theatre tickets. I immediately applied and acquired two tickets for his show at the Palladium. Danny Kaye had taken London by storm; he was sold out for every performance. I invited a girl along who at the time, I was very keen on, dear little June Rudgely. My sister was very upset that I had not taken her! I reminded her that she had seen the Ink Spots and I hadn't! I borrowed a maroon coloured v-necked sweater from her, turned it back to front, and pinned it with a small safely pin, to make it appear like a crew neck sweater. This was something that we did quite often since we never possessed more than one sweater at a time.

I took dear June home after the show to say goodnight. When having a small kiss and cuddle, the safety pin holding my sweater became unfastened, the pin digging into the back of my neck each time I went to embrace her. The discomfort got the better of me, and it became about the quickest "goodnight" I ever had with a girl! How could I tell her that I had a sweater turned back to front?

With my arm still in a sling from my accident at work, I ventured one Saturday evening into the Bethnal

Green Road restaurant, on the corner of Mansford Street; I knew practically everyone dining there. There was a boy very well-known to us, who had a beautiful scarf that everyone was admiring; it was striped in browns, beiges and golds of different tones. He hung the scarf on a coat rack. While everyone was deep in conversation, I removed the scarf in fun. Regretfully, hours later I had forgotten all about it still being inside my sling, and I went home. The following morning, there was a knock at the door. Georgie Walker was standing there. "'Ere Derek, 'ave you got Leslie Pummel's scarf?" I told him that I had and how I had forgotten all about it until I got home the previous evening. Poor George said to me, "You're a right bastard you are! I got nicked last night and 'ave to appear at Old Street!" George then explained that after the loss of the scarf, Leslie had accused everyone of taking it. Outside the restaurant, there was a dreadful commotion which resulted in dear old George being arrested and charged, for using abusive language to a police officer and disorderly conduct!

I accompanied George to Old Street Police Court to hear the charge; I stood in the public gallery as George stood before the magistrate. The charge was read out and George, in his flat monotone voice, pleaded guilty. The magistrate fined him 5s. He replied to the magistrate, "That's my bleeding dinner money your honour, 'ow am I supposed to get my lunch?" At this point the whole thing became quite hilarious, I had to stifle my laughter at the court comedy, and tears ran down my cheeks! The whole episode was so funny that

215

the London evening newspaper *The Evening News*, which had a column "Courts Day by Day", written in a humorous style, included George in the column. The columnist made it sound even funnier! How I wish I had saved that article! Might I add, that I was not the flavour of the month with dear George!

Some months later, I took George to a dance in Kensington, somewhere a little more upmarket than the East End! We were standing there, eyeing up the girls. George had just had a new suit made, and turning round to me he said in that flat monotone voice of his, "What do ya reckon Derek? I'm only the best dressed geyser 'ere in this room tonight!" George just couldn't help being full of self-esteem! He, and many others like him, were porters in Covent Garden or Spitalfields. When those markets closed down, most of them became taxi drivers. A few years later I was taking a girl out and hailed a taxi in Hackney Road, when who should the taxi driver be, but none other than dear old George! I could see George looking into the cab mirror, looking at the girl I was with; he hadn't changed one bit! Some years later, I was discussing George with one of his fellow taxi drivers, and apparently the other taxi drivers called him "Georgie Buckall". On asking why, he explained that George, who had had all his teeth extracted, had difficulty in his pronunciation, hence, instead of saying "fuck all", he could only pronounce "buck all".

CHAPTER
NINE

"In the Kate"

To be in the "Kate" is a cockney expression for being in the army; it derives from Kate Carney, a music hall star. Her name somehow found its way into the cockney vocabulary, Kate Carney rhyming with army.

Opening up the post one morning I received a letter requesting me to register at the labour exchange in Kingsland Road for National Service. Duly reporting at the appointed time and date, I was asked what arm of the service I wished to go into. Initially, I requested the Royal Navy, until I was informed that in the army one served the shortest time, so consequently I opted for the army.

A few weeks later, I received another letter, asking me to report for a medical in Burdett Road, Bow. Arriving at the centre in Burdett Road, I found it was packed with National Service fodder, many in a state of undress, arched over having their "jacksies" looked up, being prodded and poked by doctors in white coats with their badges of office, their stethoscopes around their necks. I went through this conveyor belt procedure of medical examiners, along with all the others, and was pronounced "A1".

In early December I was on a troop train to Barnard Castle in County Durham. Fortunately, one of my old school classmates from Teesdale Street School was joining the same regiment; George Brown, one of the Brown twins, who lived in Peabody Buildings, Old Bethnal Green Road. Both twins were market porters at Covent Garden, following in their father's footsteps, and were always beautifully dressed. Their brother Jimmy had been called up at the same time to the 3rd Carabiniers, another regiment of the Armoured Corps. We changed trains at Darlington, then on to Barnard Castle and were transported to the camp of the Royal Armoured Corps. The training regiment was the Prince of Wales Own 12th Royal Lancers.

We were transported from Barnard Castle Station to the barracks that held both regiment and trainee soldiers. The barracks comprised single brick buildings and Nissen huts. We were ushered into a brick building that accommodated roughly forty soldiers. A single combustion stove, situated in the centre of the room, was our only source of heating. We were a mixture of young men from all walks of life, and from all parts of the country. Here we had the extroverts, introverts, the brash, timid and the shy. Public school accents, Cockney, Geordie, Scottish; accents that you had never heard before, and some you had difficulty in understanding.

The whole day was spent being kitted out with kitbag, groundsheet, battledress, greatcoat, beret, tank suits, denim fatigue suits, boots, underwear, cutlery, jackknife and all your webbing that made up for FSMO (full service marching order). Gathering all this kit together and taking it to our barracks, we made for the dining hall and were given cards with the meals and days printed on it for a whole month; the dining hall orderly would punch a hole in our card for the meal taken on that specific day. As we trundled through this vast dining area for our very first army meal, a shout went up from the troops already dining, "You'll be sorry!" This was done with every new intake as a welcoming gesture, as we later found ourselves doing the same thing when the next new intake arrived. If ever one can remember a meal, that army meal was unforgettable. Two semi-warm sausage rolls, not flaky pastry, not shortcrust, just hardened baked flour, cold boiled potatoes and carrots swimming in tepid gravy. It was revolting but being hungry from leaving London, we had no choice other than to eat it.

Because of the goings on, running here and there, and being bestowed the rank of Trooper, with the Army No. 22091632, I hadn't sighted George until I got to the dining hall. George, who had arrived at the barracks in a smart tailored suit, was now wearing army denims; it was a terrible transformation seeing this very smart man in such awful-looking clothing! Poor old George looked so forlorn and dejected! I really felt sorry for him, not realising that I must have looked like it too!

That very first night at lights out, I lay in bed listening to some of those boys sobbing; initially I could not make out why they were crying, not realising that some had never ever been away from home before. It must have been my experience as an evacuee and living away from home that had hardened me, as no tears came forth like some of the others.

The following day we were marched to the medical centre for our vaccinations and inoculations, having four injections in all, two in each arm, one in the upper and one in the lower. We were lined up in single file, and to my amazement, some of the boys started fainting before they even got to the doctor! I really thought that this was only something they did in the movies! Amongst groups of young men brought together, there are always those who are much brighter, and those not so bright. We had one boy we called "Nig-Nog". He had a north country accent you could cut with a knife and we had difficulty understanding him. Dear old Nig-Nog was always dropping off to sleep. One night we came back from the NAAFI to our barracks to find Nig-Nog fast asleep in bed. It was bitterly cold with snow on the ground. We lifted Nig Nog, still fast asleep in his bed, and carried him out on to the pathway outside the barracks and left him there. It was two hours or more after that he finally awoke to his very odd surroundings!

Our next few weeks were spent in "square bashing" and kit-cleaning. The boots issued were brown ex-Australian army, and these had to be blackened and spit and polished. To get them totally black was no easy effort, as the brown leather shone through time and time again. It took a while to gain the "spit and polish" technique — through perseverance it gradually paid off and we were able to make those toecaps and heels really shine. Our webbing brass had never seen a polish!

Hours were spent rubbing the coarse metal to a smooth finish until it was shining. All the webbing had to be "blanco'd", and low and behold if any "blanco" was found on your brass! Our complete kit had to be laid out on our beds a million times over for inspection.

We drilled and drilled and drilled, marching up and down, rifle drill, shoulder arms, present arms, and pistol drill. It never seemed to come to an end! At any unannounced time of the evening, an NCO, with his riding crop under his arm, would order us to wear our FSMO, rifle and pistol and report to the drill sheds. This could be at ten o'clock in the evening or sometimes even later and we would drill for an hour or two. Marching drill, rifle drill and pistol drill, arriving back at our barrack room absolutely exhausted. At times you were ordered to lay your complete kit out on your bed. An NCO would come in to inspect, and seeing something not to his liking, he would pick up a boot and throw it right to the other end of the room, swearing and cussing at the poor unfortunate whose piece of equipment had not been up to standard! Whenever an NCO entered late in the evening, we knew we were in for a hard time. Reveille was sounded at 6a.m., our toilets and washhouses were 200yds away. It was a particularly cold winter, and often you would arrive for your ablutions to find the water hardly tepid. There was a bank of WC's with concrete flooring. Behind each toilet door, you would find someone had written a poem, or something crude. One I will always remember was:

Be careful how you close this door
For there's many an unborn trooper
Who is fast asleep upon this floor!

We would muster on the vast drill square each morning in our various troops. The regimental band would be playing. The RSM, wee Georgie Day, was about the smartest soldier I ever saw. He was most noticeable by his glistening brown boots! I never quite fathomed out why he could wear brown boots, when we were issued with brown boots and had to make them black! Whenever he gave an order on the square it became a high pitched screech.

Army jargon is like no other. I do not know how this particular accent came about. We would be lined up as a troop on early morning parade. A squadron sergeant would come behind you and say something like, "Am I hurting you? No? I should be, I'm standing on your bloody hair, get a bloody haircut!" even if you had your hair cut the day before! "Did you shave this morning? You forgot to take the paper off the razor blade." At times you got the impression that they were deliberately trying to humiliate you. There were some NCOs who delighted in this, and I'm convinced that some had a sadistic streak that went unchecked.

Going to the dining hall on one particular lunchtime, we could not believe our eyes. The menu was the best we had seen on camp, everything was beautifully displayed and the choice much greater than we normally had. All the cooks were in snow-white aprons, all the equipment was gleaming. It did not take too

222

long for the penny to drop that the regiment was having a high ranking officer visit the camp. The following day, and thereafter, we were back to normal.

One morning I received a freshly laundered tank suit. Not bothering to examine it, I put it on. The garment zipped from the ankle upwards on each leg to the shoulders. Standing to attention I felt a riding crop across my leg. "Did you know your tank suit is torn?" I replied, "No sir." "Another fucking liar in the regiment, double the troop around the square twelve times at the double." We doubled that vast square as ordered and all the way down to the gunnery wing, finally coming to a halt. The Squadron Sergeant shouted "Who's the c★★t who said he never knew his tank suit was torn?" "Me Sergeant," I replied. "B-o-l-l-ocks!" he yelled back at the top of his voice. Fortunately, I had no repercussions from the rest of the boys of our Gunnery Troop.

The commanding officer of the regiment was Lt. Colonel Horsberry-Porter. The only time we ever saw him was when he was riding through the camp on horseback, a very tall man always wearing a winter fur coat. Only on one occasion did we have to see him personally in his office. We were briefed by the Squadron Sergeant Major to address the Lt. Colonel as "Colonel." To make quite sure that we said "Colonel" at the end of every sentence, the SSMS gave you a prod with his riding crop. All NCOs carried a riding crop "blanco'd" white with a silver top embossed with the 12th Royal Lancers Crest, great for prodding and poking.

The "breaking us in" period from "rookie" to "soldier" was quite arduous, with all the physical exercises, drilling, boring fatigues and the actual gunnery training. The fatigues were assigned to the back of the cookhouse, with a mountain of potatoes to be peeled with hand-peelers. Nothing could be more soul-destroying than sitting there, peeling potatoes which never ever seemed to come to an end! We had the occasional film, shown in the regimental theatre, and sometimes a concert. It's funny how certain tunes remind you of a place or a person. At this particular time, "12th Street Rag" was all the rage — each time I hear it played now my thoughts immediately return to my training days with the 12th Royal Lancers.

We were given the task of carrying green wooden ammunition boxes on a particular rainy day, and were wearing greatcoats. Somehow the green dye from the boxes stained them. George and I were charged with this demeanour. We were individually marched into the Squadron Major's office. I was asked to give my account and the charge was dismissed. I waited for George to come out. "What did you get George?" "Five days jankers," said George. He then asked me what I got; I replied, "Nothing." "How the fucking hell did you get nothing?" I could not really explain to George why I got nothing and he got five days' CB! This meant he had been "confined to barracks" and had to report to the guardhouse in full service marching order (FMSO) for inspection every hour until midnight.

We had our first guard duty parade. The Duty Officer inspected us, and I was quite amazed that I was chosen as "Stick Man". The Stick Man is the smartest man on parade, selected by the duty officer. I had not the slightest idea what this meant, only that at the end of the inspection, I had to "fall out". The following morning, George and the rest of the guard returned to the barracks. "What was it like George?" I asked. "I nearly shit myself, guarding the perimeters of the camp in the dead of night," he replied. One patrolled the perimeters for two hours, then rested in all your kit for the next four, sleeping if you could on beds with just the wire springs to lie on. Weekend guard was always dreaded, having to do guard duties for forty-eight hours without taking off your uniform. At the end of the duty, you came away feeling an absolute mess.

The winter of 1948 was bitterly cold, particularly in the north, with such vast open spaces surrounding us. We were taken by truck very late at night into the middle of nowhere and dumped, given a map and a compass, and were instructed to find our way back to camp. There were about six of us in our party. I'm sure, like many others at that time, I had not a clue about map reading. We walked and walked across the countryside, absolutely frozen, finding a barn where we rested for a few hours, out of the cold. Eventually, through sheer luck, we found our way back to camp, arriving at the barracks with my hands so frozen I could not unbutton my greatcoat until I warmed them close to the combustion stove for several minutes when they thawed out.

We were given Christmas leave bang in the middle of our training. Arriving back at Bethnal Green in uniform, I felt rather proud of our Royal Armoured Corps red and yellow shoulder flashes, the red and yellow denoting "Death before Dishonour" and the silver cap badge of the Mailed Fist and Crown. One attempted to pack in as much as you possibly could during those few days, before returning to Barnard Castle. We visited Barry's, where most of us then were all in uniform, as well as having plenty of Christmas parties to attend.

To return to camp was always a wrench, travelling back north on a crowded troop train. I don't think I ever got a seat returning from leave in the whole time I was in England. From Barnard Castle Station, we had a shortcut across the fields to the camp; there was hardly any time left before drawing your kit out, and your hands and face were filthy from the grime and soot of the train. We then had to get washed and changed for early morning parade which was always a race against time.

It was then back to the gunnery wing, learning more about the armament of our Daimler armoured cars and the ammunition that the two-pounders and 7.92 Besa machine guns would fire. We were also trained to judge distances, study range-finding and map reading, all of which was to turn us into first-class crew members of an armoured car. Halfway through our training we were sent to Appleby in Northumberland for actual shooting on the firing ranges from armoured cars.

I was teamed up with another boy, Howard, who, strangely enough, had worked for Windsmoor in Old Street, where my sister was currently working. At least we had a little something in common. We were fairly cramped inside the turret of a Daimler armoured car, having only the breech of the gun separating us. Howard was designated to load the shells, and I was to do the firing. Placing the shell into the breach, I aimed at the target and pulled the trigger. Nothing happened. I cocked the gun again and fired again, nothing happened. At this stage, and it was becoming quite scary as the shell could explode in the breach, I suspected that we had a dud one. Should anything like this occur, you are to remove the shell and throw it out of the turret. I attempted this one more time, re-cocked and fired again but still nothing happened. My gun loader started shouting, "Oh quick — Oh quick — Oh, quick." Opening up the breech, I removed the shell and threw it out of the turret, with a great sigh of relief. This was our baptism into using live ammunition, a hair-raising first time experience!

Our quarters in Appleby were quite spartan. Sleeping in a Nissen hut with a single stove, it was a cold and desolate place to be in winter. We were pleased when our gunnery was over and we were able to return to camp. One morning the whole regiment was mustered at very short notice to the parade ground. We all thought that we were going to be shipped out to Korea. There were a thousand men on the square, waiting to be addressed by the colonel. He began his speech by saying, "You call yourselves Englishmen, I am disgusted with you!" We had not the faintest idea what he was talking about. We all marched to the other side of the camp, and were ordered to pass through a shower unit where someone had crapped in a shower cubicle! The excitement of being posted overseas went out of the window.

Grandmother had sent me one of her homemade cakes. When I was at home I hardly ever touched her creations. This time it was most welcome. I shared it with several of the boys, without any complaint. We were forever hungry; most of our money was spent on food in the NAAFI during the evenings. Our pay during training was 10s one week, £1 the next. Pay parade was quite a performance. To collect your 10s or a £1 you marched to the pay desk; two paces forward, saluted, collected your money, about turned and marched off!

We were given forty-eight hours leave, with travel warrants. Prior to going on leave, an NCO would come to inspect us and the barracks. We would stand by our beds, blankets folded around the three biscuit mattresses, and if the NCO was satisfied with your appearance and bed layout, you were allowed to proceed on leave. George was facing me on the opposite side. I had been inspected and was OK, but poor old George had cut himself shaving, and had to remain in barracks for the weekend. I was asked to pass a message on to his girlfriend when I got home, to say he was sorry he couldn't make it.

Most of the boys I knew had been called up for National Service. It was amazing to find how many of them managed to get around prolonging a leave, and how the word spread as to how to do it! There was a doctor in Nichol Square known as Black Joe who, for a

£1, would issue you with a certificate to state that you were too sick to return to your unit. There were times when I had been sorely tempted to pay Black Joe a visit, but never got around to doing so.

Arriving back in London, it seemed that no sooner were you there, than your forty-eight hours' leave was over! I returned back to camp once again from Euston by troop train, sleeping in the corridor of a carriage, smoke-filled and grimy. Alighting from the train at Barnard Castle in the early hours of the morning and walking across the fields, I felt like nothing on earth, due to not having a proper night's sleep. I lined up with all the others to collect my kit and no sooner had I got back to my barracks, when the bugle sounded for parade. I had no time to wash, just spruced myself up as best as I could. My face and hands were still grimy from the train. So, on noting this, the inspecting NCO ordered me to the bathrooms under escort, after the parade was over. I had to strip, bathe in a bath tub of ice-cold water, with a scrubbing brush that was meant for the floor. It was a most degrading and humiliating experience and I never, ever, forgot it. At times the army could be downright stupid; there was no one you could address or turn to when you felt an injustice had been done in those days.

On the finalization of our training we had to take all our kit up on to the parade ground and lay it out on ground sheets for inspection. Everything had to be boxed square, with cardboard placed inside; rather a fruitless task as, when the inspection was over, the cardboard was thrown away!

The final day came for the Passing Out Parade, the one that we had been drilling for all this time. The 12th Royal Lancers regimental band was on the square to play through the whole event. The regiment's Lt. Colonel took the salute on horseback, as, by this time, we were fully conditioned soldiers. There was a great sigh of relief when all the drilling, gunnery course, fatigues and being barked and shouted at, had come to an end. Four of us, George included, had our photograph taken at the end of the passing out parade. I made a casual remark saying, "I wonder what we will look like?" I didn't realise that the Squadron Sergeant Major was standing behind me. He said "I'll tell you what you bloody well look like!"

Our Gunnery Sergeant asked me if I would like to stay on to become a gunnery instructor with the 12th Royal Lancers. I felt quite flattered; I never recognized that I had the capability of becoming an instructor. However, since most of the postings after training were abroad, I declined. The urge to travel far out-weighed anything else. We were mustered outside HQ and addressed by the SSM who read out the regiments that we were assigned to. The majority of us were posted to the 13th/18th Hussars stationed in North Africa, and the 1st Royal Dragoons (The Royals) which were stationed in Germany. George and I were posted to occupied Germany.

It was all very exciting as I had never travelled abroad before. We travelled by train from the north of England to Harwich, crossing over to the Hook of Holland by sea, then by train to Brunswick in

Germany. Everywhere was full of interest to me, passing through Holland to Aachen at the German border, and through several German cities which were still in ruins from the war. Deutschland had not quite got back on its feet at this time — there was still much rebuilding to be done.

The barracks of the 1st Royal Dragoons were based at Wolfenbutel, just a few kilometres from Braunschweig. They were the finest I had ever seen! Built for the German army, they put ours back home to shame, and were constructed in a square of grey stone, solid as a rock and made to last. The regiment was divided into three squadrons, "HQ", "B" and "C"; "A" Squadron was based in Berlin. We were assigned to "C" Squadron, and were quartered in rooms of four. Centrally heated, with double windows, we could not believe our good fortune at the wonderful transformation from the austere living accommodation at Barnard Castle to this! The immediate front part of the square was a huge archway, above it the officers' quarters, and either side was HQ Squadron admin and "MT" (motor transport). To the right of the square was "C" Squadron and to the left "B" Squadron. At the far end leading up a stone staircase was the recreation area comprising the NAAFI and the library. In the centre of the inner square was a very pleasant cultivated garden.

We were taken to the regimental tailor, chalked and pinned up, the surplus material in our uniforms taken out, making us much smarter soldiers than when we arrived. The dining arrangements of the regiment were excellent; we were served by German waitresses, such a far cry from our training days! The standards were very high, so high in fact, that one of the cooks who was in the army catering corps, got five days' CB for burning the bacon!

Our immediate programme was drilling — rifle drill and pistol drill — for yet another Passing Out Parade as a 1st Royal Dragoon. It seemed child's play in comparison to what we had been through with the 12th Royal Lancers. Perhaps too, at this stage, we were more conditioned and disciplined. Our Lt. Colonel, Rodney Heathcote-Amory, took the salute, addressing us as Gentlemen Dragoons of the Royals. It was a fine regiment; you were made to feel you belonged, and I felt rather proud to be part of it. The regiment was steeped in history; it was the first cavalry regiment formed by Charles I, and then known as the "Tangier Horse", dating back to 1660.

We were taken to see the regimental silver, displayed on a very large, highly-polished refectory table, in the officers' mess. It was a most magnificent sight; I had never seen so many beautiful silver pieces put together under one roof, really intricate craftsmanship which had been donated to the regiment over the years. One piece that stood out above all others was a blue enamelled silver cigarette case, with a circle of diamonds with the initial "W" also in diamonds in the centre. My inquisitive nature led me to ask who had presented it to the regiment. It had apparently been donated by Kaiser Wilhelm, who was at one time an Honorary Colonel in Chief of the regiment.

Each Thursday was Colonels' night; trumpeters would come on to the balcony outside the officers' mess, to play a fanfare: officers would dine in mess kit, and the whole evening would be a very impressive affair. We would stand and watch the trumpeters play practically every time we were in barracks.

We began the second part of our training to become fully fledged gunner mechanics (gunner drivers) by initially driving fifteen cwt Bedford trucks up and down the autobahn, then on to the AFV's (armoured fighting vehicles) across rough terrain, putting us through our paces. The driving position in those vehicles was a centre steering, you were almost stretched out on the floor. In the summer, encased in steel armour, it became very hot. Driving miles on the autobahn, it was very easy to fall off to sleep. Fortunately, you had a car commander, who was able to jolt you back over the intercom system! On night manoeuvres we were not allowed to use any lights other than follow the rear small red light of the car in front of you. We were out on manoeuvres one night, with George in the car in front of me. His car commander was a Lieutenant Farraday, who could not pronounce his r's. Following a small red light for hours was not an easy task, and the Lieutenant was shouting at poor old George, "Bwown, Bwown, what the bloody hell are you doing?" Quite apart from the difficulty in driving on these night schemes, it did have its humorous side. George and I were in the turret of an armoured car one day, when he turned around and said to me, "You know, if my mum saw me in one of these things she would cry her fucking eyes out." Finally, on passing all our tests we were transferred to "B" Squadron. We did further gunnery on the firing ranges at Belsen, a name that will never be forgotten. Most of the camp by now held displaced persons from all over Europe.

Barrack room life in "B" Squadron was good. Sleeping only four to a room, the squadron held our interest in forever being involved in various activities, keeping us constantly on the alert. The time came for the efficiency tests, where we route marched in FSMO, then ran in FSMO. When you ran, the camouflage netting of your helmet resting against your forehead stung like hell, possibly from the preserving agent of the netting. With your full pack, rifle and stinging helmet, running behind a truck and being timed was quite an exhausting exercise.

Most evenings, when not on duty, were spent having a glass of beer in the NAAFI at the far end of the barracks. The German beer supplied to the regiment was very good, and on a hot summer's day it could be quite refreshing. Coming out of the NAAFI one evening with George, we stood on the stone steps of the terrace. There was a full moon. George said to me, "You see that moon? They can see that moon back home! What would you be doing now if you were home?" I replied that I would most probably be at Barry's. George then said, "I would be with my bird." We stood there gazing up at the moon in silence, both wrapped up in our own thoughts of home. Although George would appear to be a hard nut, I came to the conclusion that deep down, he really was a softy and a romantic.

Sitting in our room one evening, I was reading the *Hackney Gazette* that my grandmother used to send, along with a cake, on a regular basis. When one of the boys came in and observed what I was reading, he asked, "Christ, you don't live there, do you?" He had noticed the front page of the *Gazette* with its crime articles. Up to this point, it had never struck me how other people viewed those of us who lived in the East End. I could not see anything untoward in the paper; it was something I was used to, but I re-read the front page, to see what he was so disturbed about. I then explained to him what life was like, and that it was not as bad as it appeared in print. To an outsider it must have looked horrendous.

Germany then was still recovering; cigarettes and coffee were the main trading commodities. A pound of coffee would go a long way — a maid could be hired for a week for the price of a jar of Nescafé! You would see men of the Control Commission (CCG) in their dark navy blue-dyed battledress and berets everywhere, trading with the locals. It was a black market paradise. We had a regimental dance on one occasion; half the local girls arrived from Wolfenbutel, wearing coats made from army blankets! Thank God we never froze!

We were never paid in Deutschmarks, but in "BAFFS", army currency. However, by trading in little odds and ends, we were able to obtain the mark for our personal purchases. We were in the British Zone of Occupied Germany (BAOR). Overlooking us was the

Russian Zone; they were in a position to turn off our water supply at the drop of a hat, but fortunately, they never did. The relationship between the Allies and the Russians at this particular time was not exactly cordial. Our purpose in being there was to patrol the Russian Zone border between Helmstedt and Bad Hartzburg in the Hartz Mountains. We would be away from camp for three to four days at a time under canvas.

On one of our patrols into the mountains, I did not feel too well and as time wore on I felt increasingly worse. I could hardly swallow and my head was aching. Lasting out until we got back to camp, I went to the mess. If there is one thing I hate, it is the smell of boiled fish. This happened to be on the menu, and the very smell of it made me feel worse. I left the mess hall fairly rapidly, returned to my room and went to bed. The following morning I felt so ill that I reported sick. The army had a wonderful system when you reported sick; you placed all your kit into storage. I hardly had the strength to lift up a boot lace, let alone my whole kit. However, I managed to do everything one should under such circumstances, but with great difficulty. Reporting to the medical centre, as it was Easter, I found the regimental doctor was away for the weekend, so a local German doctor was called in. I was sent to bed in the hospital immediately. When it came to mealtime, the orderly brought my food in and when I lifted up the chop cover, I found it was boiled fish! I could have died from the smell alone! The following morning, I was taken by military ambulance to the military hospital in Hanover, having been diagnosed, inaccurately, as having diphtheria.

I was placed in a ward all by myself and given penicillin injections in the behind by a huge, and not so gentle, German nurse. She looked more like a Hausefrau than a nurse! After a week of rest and regular injections in what was by then a very sore backside, I returned to camp, having recovered from a very nasty bout of tonsillitis. It was something in my younger years that I used to get quite frequently, but after my treatment in Germany, I never had a reoccurrence.

One day, looking at the regimental notice, I saw that a ration clerk was required. I applied and was interviewed by the regimental Quarter Master and got the job, a nice relief from soldiering! I struck up a friendship with our regimental German barber, and now and then, gave him some cocoa powder. One evening, on Colonels' night, when all the officers were out on the balcony, I passed, giving a very smart salute, but bringing my arm down with such a slam that it broke open the secreted packet of cocoa! However the powder fortunately dispersed over the side of my uniform, away from the officers who were looking down from the balcony. I narrowly escaped being placed on a "fizzer" (a charge). We supplied all the married families in the area with rations, and everything had to be worked out by fractions. Some of the wives would become terribly flirtatious in order to acquire extra rations, and other wives would complain. I was not terribly good at working out allowances in fractions then, so it resulted in married soldiers' wives complaining to the QM. I really should have known better!

Come Armistice Day, the regiment held a parade, with the regimental band marching down to Wolfenbutel. Shortly before going on parade, I was filling a cigarette lighter from a gelatine capsule, when some of the petrol dropped on to the toe of my boot, leaving a small dull patch. The inspection came and I was duly charged with having dirty boots. Going through the procedure of left, right, left, right, I was marched in to the Squadron Major, where I explained my mishap and was given five days CB (jankers). CB entailed you reporting to the guardhouse, in FSMO (full service marching order) for inspection several times a day. I volunteered for the boxing team, and was consequently excused from reporting to the guardhouse, and in between training, was ordered to work in the officers' mess for the five days', which I did not object to in the slightest!

The regiment had a strange way of getting together a boxing team in a rapid spell of time, but was nevertheless most effective. The whole regiment of OR's was lined up in two single files; the soldier facing you was your opponent, no matter how big or small, large or lean. You would then enter the ring for three minutes, and knock the hell out of each other; I lasted for about three or four bouts, finally getting knocked out in the fifth session. The line would gradually be reduced, until you had enough candidates to form a regimental boxing team!

I was then shifted to Administration in HQ, to spend the rest of my army days in a very pleasant office working out the guard duties for the regiment. A very nice number and surprising how popular I became! Now and again, we were given various duties outside the normal routine. One day, right out of the blue, six of us in HQ were ordered to draw rifles and fifty rounds of ammunition, without any details given. We were told to muster at 22.00 hrs, still without any knowledge of what we were about to do. At the given time, we were picked up by a truck, and taken into the middle of nowhere, to a railwayman's hut at the side of a railway track.

Our NCO then briefed us. We were to pick up a train that was going to Berlin. It was our task to see that all blinds were drawn, the carriage doors locked throughout the journey, and that no Russians were to be allowed on the train. The relationship between the Allies and the Russians was extremely volatile. I asked the NCO what we should do if any Russians attempted to board the train. We were informed that we should hit them with the butt of the rifle, but not to shoot!

The train slowed down at our meeting point, we boarded and were stationed along the carriages, checking each compartment to see that the blinds were drawn, as it had been known for the Russians to shoot if they weren't. We arrived at the checkpoint with uniformed Russians very much in evidence. I stood between the carriages and could not believe my eyes as there were no bolts on the carriage door! A very tall Russian officer, with two soldiers, came along and attempted to open the door next to where I was standing. I held it with all the strength I could muster. I could not visualize myself hitting three Russians with the butt of my rifle! With good fortune, they realised I was not allowing them to board the train, and moved on. It was a nerve-wracking episode. The train was allowed to proceed through the Russian Zone to Berlin. At Magdeburg, it slowed down to a walking pace. The station was crowded with Russian soldiers, and it was evident that they had been enjoying the wee small hours! I fully expected, observing the condition that many of them were in, that some might take a pot shot if one of the train travellers was silly enough to raise their blind. It was with a great sigh of relief when we passed through unhindered. We arrived in Berlin very tired, but not too tired to see as much of Berlin as we could!

During the following month I was selected, with five others, to go by train to Oldenburg to pick up a new supply of armoured cars. We were given a guard's van with bunks, and a stove for cooking our meals. A journey by road to Oldenburg was only a matter of hours away, but this journey took us four days. We were shunted and shoved, moved into sidings in goods' yards, and took turns to cook the main meal of the day from the compo rations we were supplied with. I decided to make a stew, my very first attempt at cooking! Not being very experienced, I placed too much potato powder into my concoction which resulted in it being so thick, you could cut it like a cake! I gave it away to a German railway guard who was with us throughout; he thought it was very good! Those few days were very hot and sunny, and I climbed to the top of the guards' van to sunbathe. On the roof, I saw something that drew my attention. It was a lady's pistol, wrapped in a handkerchief. I wondered what mysteries this gun held, and why had someone wrapped it in a handkerchief. I could only think that it must have had some sinister history. For a while, I decided to keep it, so I cleaned it up, and made it workable again. Returning with the armoured cars to the regiment, my conscience got the better of me, and I decided to hand it in to the armoury, thus relieving me of any complications!

It was not too long after picking up the armoured cars in Oldenburg that we were named yet again and placed on a religious course at Verden. The course entailed religious studies, towards becoming confirmed. However we had not the slightest inkling that we were to be confirmed until our arrival at the religious centre. This was a lovely country house, set in several wooded acres, very restful with an air of serenity about it. After a few days, the atmosphere of the place seemed to envelop me into a cocoon of theology. It had me thinking so deeply, I felt on the brink of taking up the priesthood. It was only the influence of the others from the regiment, who were not as affected as I, which brought me back down to earth, severing the spiritual feelings that had so engrossed me. Quite possibly, it must have been the ambience and tranquillity of the place that had made me feel this way. Come the day of the confirmation, it was a mass production service at a

church in Verden, conducted by the Bishop of
Croydon, chaplain to the army. We army personnel
were lined up in double file. I knelt before the Bishop
with an ATS girl alongside me to take the bread and
wine. Of all the confirmations I had attended back
home, I had never ever experienced one like this, on
such a grand scale.

Returning to the regiment, I found that I was due to
go on leave after ten months away — it was a strange
feeling, knowing you were going home after so long. We
had our new cap badge issued. It was, in fact, the
original type but had been changed in wartime because
it looked too much like the German eagle. It was rather
odd as when I did arrive home in uniform, and I was
walking down Old Bethnal Green Road, I heard a
young boy say to his mother "Look Mum, a German!"
To put on a civilian suit again felt like you had nothing
on your back. It was virtually weightless! It was lovely
to visit the old haunts, say hello to the neighbours, go
to Barry's, and meet up with old friends.

To eke out my soldier's pay, and to have a little more
money to spend during my leave, I got a casual labour
job at Mann & Crossman's brewery in Mile End Road.
It was back-breaking work, stacking beer crates a mile
high, for £1 a day. There were occasions when you had
to pass through the bottling department, staffed
entirely by women who would whistle and shout at you!
I literally raced through that department, as stories
abounded whereby those brewery wenches would grab
you, take your trousers down, and put boot blacking
around your nether regions, as part of a little

excitement in their daily lives, so giving you an initiating ceremony for venturing into their domain! Those ladies were hardly the sophisticated types. Each evening, I would arrive home with every bone in my body aching; it was about the hardest physical work I had ever done. Within the shadow of the Mann & Crossman brewery is the Blind Beggar public house which became the most famous, or infamous, when on the night of 9 March 1966, Ronnie Kray went in with one of his cohorts and shot George Cornell three times in the head. The public house is now a byword for the East End.

Who was the "Blind Beggar"? The Blind Beggar of Bethnal Green was, and is, the symbol and legend of Bethnal Green. His story became clouded in myth. It was at a time long before Bethnal Green became a chaotic and overcrowded slum in the nineteenth century. It was first mentioned in an eighth-century deed. By the Middle Ages it was rather isolated from London, being just a small and rather grand little village. There were manor houses and mansions in the surrounding countryside and cottages clustered around the green itself. In the 1200s, one of those manor houses belonged to Simon de Montfort. The story of how he went from rich noble to a poor beggar was recounted in Percy's *Reliques of Ancient English Poetry*. The tale went on to become a popular part of folklore during Tudor times. Simon was a soldier in the service of the King, and fought at the Battle of Evesham, in the West Country, in 1265. Legend has it that he fell at the battle and was

243

found, blinded and wandering by a nobleman's daughter who nursed him back to health; during the course of his recovery, they fell in love and wed. In time they had a daughter and named her Besse. Besse was very beautiful but could not find a husband, the problem being her father. Besse was courted by four suitors: a rich gentleman, a knight, a London merchant and an innkeeper's son. Most of them withdrew their suit when they met Montfort to ask for the old soldier's consent to marriage. Montfort's reduced circumstances were related through a popular song at the time:

> My father, shee said, is soone to be seene,
> The siely, blind beggar of Bednall-greene,
> That daylye sits begging for charitie,
> He is the good father of pretty Besse
> Hei makrs and tokens are known very well;
> He always is led with a dog and bell
> A seely old man, God knoweth is he,
> Yet he is the father of pretty Besse

In a predictable medieval twist, the courtly knight was the only man who could see past the seeming lack of decent dowry to the woman he loved. He received his reward, as the couple were given a dowry of £3,000, plus £100 for Besse's wedding dress.

It was now May 1950 and I was due to return to the regiment from my leave. Grandfather insisted on coming to Liverpool Street station to see me off.

244

Reluctantly, I agreed. Waiting for the train to Harwich, I was in conversation with him leaning up against a column. In the station, a Redcap (military police) came over and cautioned me for doing so. Grandfather took exception to this. "Who the bleeding hell does he think he's talking to?" I had to calm him down, thinking that if he didn't behave, I would be returning to barracks and facing a charge!

Arriving back at the regiment in Germany, it was only a matter of weeks before we were due to be "demobbed". In fact, that was all our minds were focused on. At long last came the day when we were to say goodbye to the army. We were interviewed prior to our departure, and asked if we would like to sign on as regulars. I don't think any of us did. Looking back on the whole period, I have never, for one moment, resented it. It did more good than anything else; there were, of course, ugly periods but they were soon forgotten, and all in all, it instilled a sense of pride in one's self, and gave a person backbone and self-discipline.

Finally, returning to England on a train, racing across Germany and Holland, I sat in the railway carriage, my thoughts churning, wondering what on earth I was going to do with my life. I had not the slightest idea what career I would like follow. For the past year and a half, I had not needed to worry about myself, but was now faced with the dilemma of my future. The train and boat crossing to the demobilisation centre in Colchester seemed to take an eternity. Finally, we arrived to hand in all our kit,

245

which was in a much better condition than when we received it! We were divested of all our insignia. Eventually arriving in Bethnal Green, I was back home at No. 74.

CHAPTER
TEN

A Return to Civilian Life

At home there was now only Grandmother, Grandfather and myself. It took a little time to readjust after army life, but gradually, I began to settle back into the old lifestyle. Not knowing what to do with my life still persisted, and I was yet to find the answer. After a couple of weeks' leave, I began searching for a job. Through acquaintances I found casual work that suited me fine until I decided on my future. The job was at Foster's in Queensbridge Road. They were mainly a transport firm that had contracts with the Times Furnishing Company, and a separate division for the government's Ministry of Works.

During the war the government had requisitioned numerous properties around London for offices, some in the most salubrious areas. New government buildings were now being built to replace those they had requisitioned, and in order to return them to the original owners most of the old office furniture had been removed and taken to a depot in Neasden for selling off. The new buildings were, in most cases, furnished with brand new office furniture.

Foster's Yard, as we knew it, engaged a body of casual labour, although not so casual when you think some of them had been with the firm for a number of years. If ever there was a bunch of loveable rogues, they were it! Most of them had been in the armed forces, although some were deserters. If the yard was paid an official visit by police or Redcaps, the ones on the run would scurry over the wall! Practically every one of them gambled; travelling to a job they would be in the back of the van playing cards, as well as at lunchtime, and going home! Racing papers would be read — whether it be dogs or horses. The conversation would always be the bets they had placed, the horses that lost by a nose, and the prices they came in on. Their whole world revolved around gambling and racing; it was all horses and dogs. By strange coincidence, one of the drivers was the boy, Lenny Ebbs, with whom I had been evacuated.

We were divided into two crews. Those in one building would deal with the outgoing furniture, and those at the other end who would receive the incoming furniture. If you were on the outgoing team, it meant that you were in a position to earn, but if you were unfortunate to be on the receiving team there would be angst. However, you took it all in your stride, accepting the good with the bad. The opposite crew could always detect if you had "had it off". They watched what you smoked and what you ate, and if the cigarettes or the meal was more expensive than the norm, you then received envious remarks.

The humour and banter were constant; it was real good old cockney humour! We had one character called "Holly", which was an abbreviation of his surname. If we were in an office shifting filing cabinets, Holly would place a florin (2s piece) on the floor, and exclaim out loud in front of the clerical staff, "Blimey, look what I found!" The staff would look up with an expression of "I wonder if it was mine?" On one occasion when he did this, it backfired — a woman claimed that it was hers! We had an awful job convincing her that it was all done in fun! One of the other boys, I refer to them as boys, they were in fact very mature men, Dick Kelly, did the chippying (carpentry). Dick could throw his voice like a ventriloquist; he would yell out "Charlie" in the office, and everyone would look around. Dick was quite an amusing character to observe, blond to greying hair, a thin pencil moustache, with a very tiny hand-rolled cigarette in the corner of his mouth. He was not exactly eloquent but would make me smile at times, by some of the words he used! If he thought something was silly, he would say "bleaten 'diculous", not "bleeding ridiculous".

Foster's of course was very good at furnishing our homes! Some of the office furniture, glass cabinets, arm chairs and settees not considered good enough for their new offices were discarded. They would fetch a beautiful price today! My grandmother's house benefited greatly in having a settee for the parlour, top quality lino in the kitchen and a few other items which enhanced her home!

At every lunchbreak, the cards would come out for a game of rummy. I became quite adept at this game, learning, of course, from some very skilled players. Money was always on the table. If we were in the Westminster area, we would use a café dubbed "Hell's Kitchen", a huge place where the food was good and the prices very reasonable.

Our work took us all over London. On one occasion, when we were working quite close to St James theatre, Orson Welles came walking past. I could not think of his name at the time; he was dressed exactly as he was in *The Third Man*. I shouted out "Look there's Harry Lime!" He was appearing at the St James in Othello. Sadly, that theatre is no longer there. Another time, we were working behind Victoria Palace and noticed Sally Ann Howells and other stars going into the rear entrance of the theatre. I followed in, quite sneakily, and was privileged to watch the rehearsals of the Royal Command Variety Performance, managing to see and hear Gracie Fields singing! Patricia Morrison was also there, she was appearing in *Kiss Me Kate*. I said to her, "I haven't got an autograph book, so kiss me Kate." She replied, "You've got something there." They must have thought that I was one of the stage hands.

Once, we were on a job in Old Street, in a typing pool. It had been raining for days. One afternoon, water was seen coming through the ceiling quite heavily. Typists were sitting there with rainwater dripping on to them! We went above to investigate, and found that there was a flat roof, that had been completely stripped of its lead covering. We never found out who did it, but lead at this time was at a premium — it was a very sought-after commodity that fetched a very good price. It was known in the East End as "blue". At another job in Whitehall, facing Downing Street, I was moving furniture down a stone staircase that had lead runners. After a couple of times moving up and down the stairs, I noticed the lead runners had gone. "The phantom has struck again!"

On Fridays after work, some of us would make for the York Hall Baths to take a bath. It was the usual performance of requesting a towel and that wretched little piece of soap that hardly ever lathered. I look back now, and recall with horror of having to put on the same work clothes to go home in! I always felt dirty immediately as I got dressed. However, it was a much better option than facing a bath in the scullery at home!

If I decided not to go out on a Saturday night, I would stay at home in the company of my grandmother. On Saturday nights, she would lay all the cutlery out on the dinner table, it was never referred to as the dining table, and proceed to "bluebell" polish and emery cloth the tableware. By this time, she had changed from keeping canaries to having budgerigars. The bird would be hopping around on the table and was able to speak, sounding very much like her! She would call him "pretty Joey" and he would reply, "pretty Joey". I would give grandmother a treat by going to Gosset Street to Annie's for fish and chips, and buy a bottle of stout for her as well. If, after the meal

251

there was music on the wireless, I would dance her around the kitchen!

Our social life was centred around dancing and the cinema. Barry's would be frequented at least two to three times a week. The Royal in Tottenham mid-week, one of the town halls on Saturday nights, and Sunday nights it would be the Lyceum in the Strand, or on occasions, Oxford House in Bethnal Green. One night, a group of us were travelling back from the Lyceum in The Strand, not being rowdy by any means, just being generally humorous. At this particular time, there was a radio show called *PC. 49* with Brian Reece. His favourite saying was, "Evening all." On reaching Liverpool Street station, a very big City of London policeman got on to our bus, and stood on the platform. Amongst our group were the two Stanleys, one big, one small. Both were weightlifters, had fine physiques and shared the same Christian name. I was sitting at the lower front end of the bus, and using the Dick Kelly technique of voice throwing, I shouted "Off you go 49!" The constable, on hearing this, promptly grabbed big Stanley and made him get off the bus with him when it stopped at Great Eastern Street! I never got around to asking Stanley what that PC did to him!

The family had a funeral to attend. It was my Aunt Phyllis's, Grandfather's sister-in-law. She lived in Somerford Street, a street that always appeared so miserable and drab. Grandmother approached me, asking me if I would lend my grandfather my pair of black shoes to attend the funeral. It resulted in my having to grace the funeral wearing brown shoes. It reminded me of the song by Stanley Holloway, "Brown boots, I ask yer"! Come the day of the funeral, all the relatives had gathered in Aunt Phyllis's small terraced house. There were bottles of beer on the table, which resulted in my Aunt Marie's face looking like the Idris advert; being a Salvationist she looked on such things with disdain! The coffin was being led out of the house, relatives were sobbing and weeping, when suddenly my grandmother's voice was heard. Stopping the procession of the relatives, she told them that they were walking out in the wrong order. The sobbing and weeping stopped immediately. The coffin and relatives returned to their original positions, regrouped and started off again, in the correct order, much to grandmother's satisfaction! The sobbing and the weeping commenced again, almost to order! The funeral over with, all the family gathered in a pub in Brady Street. Two detectives in the bar approached me, and questioned me about the tie I was wearing. They thought it was one of the Guard's regiments, until I convinced them that the dimensions of the red and blue stripes were narrower than the regimental tie. I do believe they would have arrested me for posing as a Guardsman! During this time, the conversation amongst my relatives had become very heated. I could not fathom out for a while what it was all about, until my grandfather arose from his seat, as mad as hell. The relatives were already dividing up what Aunt Phyllis had left behind, even before she had been laid to rest. Grandfather had really lost his rag, calling them "a lot of vultures". We left the pub in total silence. It was a long time before things were cordial again. I wonder how many families have relatives, hovering like vultures ready to swoop, directly the departed have left this earth, to get their hands on the spoils.

Walking down Bethnal Green Road one evening, I noticed several people entering Wilmot Street. Curiosity getting the better of me, and I found that they were all going to Wilmot Street School. A political meeting was being held there with Sir Oswald Moseley speaking. I had not seen this man since the outbreak of war when he had held an enormous rally in Ridley Road market. I went in and sat down for the entire meeting, listening to what he and other speakers had to say. It was no longer anti-Semitic; they had shifted their agenda to the blacks and immigration. There was no question about it, Moseley was a brilliant politician and orator who had served in both the Conservative and Labour Parties, but who became disillusioned with party policies, and founded the British Union of Fascists. The man had both charisma and an oratorical skill that was capable of mesmerising the masses to have them eating out of the palm of his hand. Although I admired in him the way in which he could sway his audience, I could not agree or admire his political agenda. In the whole of the audience, there was only one black man. He asked Sir Oswald what he intended doing with the blacks, if his party obtained power. Moseley replied that he would compensate them, and request them to leave the country. I could not help but feel sorry for this lone coloured person, addressing this powerful personality on a very sensitive issue, but admired him for having the courage to face up to him directly, in a sea of white faces. At the conclusion of this meeting, I reentered Bethnal Green Road towards the Salmon & Ball where there was a small public house, The Ship, where I decided to have a quiet glass of ale. Who should enter the pub but Moseley with his henchman. Somehow or the other, they thought that I was with their group, and rounds of drinks were bought that I had not the slightest objection to! I had the opportunity to speak briefly to Moseley about non-political matters and began listening more intently to the general conversation that followed. I realised that they had placed "planters" in the audience, which made me aware for the very first time how corrupt politics can be.

One morning I received a letter marked OHMS. On opening it, I found that I had been called back into the army as a "Z Reservist" with the 1st County of London Yeomanry (The Rough Riders) for further training. Reporting to Colchester, I was surprised to see an old East End associate, taking photographs of those who had been called up and back in uniform. Nosher Mason was now a "smudger" (photographer) and had wasted no time in seeing an opportunity; he very kindly took my picture and sent me a complimentary photograph.

We were kitted out, assembled and transported to Thetford in Norfolk to be quartered under canvas for two weeks' training. With typical army efficiency, I had been posted to a tank regiment, having been trained in armoured cars. Someone in Whitehall had done their work well! There were several other men with similar backgrounds, which resulted in our being sent to the transport section of the regiment. It was very spartan, living under canvas. Our ablutions were out in the open, and only with cold water taps. Our "messing" was under marquees with field kitchens to cook the meals. Dining one day, I used a Dick Kelly technique from Foster's, of throwing the voice, and said in a very army officer clipped accent, "Now just a few words chaps!" Everyone under the marquee put down their knives and forks, looked up and awaited the forthcoming speech that never occurred! It was my cockney sense of humour coming out I guess!

Men were stationed along the roadside on guard. On one occasion a visiting brigadier stopped his staff car, and asked one of the soldiers what he was guarding. "Don't know, Sir," came the reply. So much for the Z call-up! We partook in night manoeuvres, and were stuck in a wood with live ammunition being used on us, feeding off dehydrated rations, those awful powdered and dried vegetables that you submerged into boiling water! I was more than pleased to see the end of that exercise!

Our tent was infested with earwigs. They were everywhere; each time you picked up an article of clothing, you would see them running out! Some nights we managed to go into Thetford to have a drink at one of the local pubs. It was not unusual to place your hand in your pocket to buy a round of drinks, to find the little buggers running around in the palm of your hand amongst the coins!

Returning to civilian life after two weeks of wasting the tax payer's money, it was back to Foster's, for how long I knew not. We had a very big job at newly-built offices in Kensington, Charles House. Every piece of furniture installed was brand spanking new. Carrying up some huge tables to the top floor, I suddenly felt a sharp pain in my groin. The pain lasted for a few days, then gradually went away. I thought no more of it.

Two to three times a week, my evenings were spent going dancing at Barry's. He introduced my friend Terry and me to a couple of middle-aged, wealthy Americans, and asked us if we would like to show them around the sights in the East End. The Americans had the most beautiful American car that they had brought over with them. An American vehicle was a rarity in the East End at this time; the car was an absolute show stopper. Its cream bodywork sparkled, and its chrome fittings gleamed. Whenever the car was parked, it automatically drew people like a magnet. Terry and I felt like the "bee's knees", sitting in the backseat on upholstered white leather, being driven around the East End. We took these Americans to all the popular pubs where there was entertainment. As the evening progressed it became apparent to us that these men were gay. We realised during the course of the evening that Barry had set us up, since neither of us was that way inclined. We conveniently bid our adieus rather abruptly before the night had ended. We were forever weary of Barry after this episode, but continued being regular attendees to his establishment.

257

One of the boys who frequented Barry's at this time was Dennis Stafford. I knew him as Dennis Seigenberg. He was a shy, reticent, good-looking young man, softly spoken, polite and always impeccably dressed. On odd occasions we dated the same girl. Lovely, slender, blue-eyed Rose, who lived just off of Dalston Junction. Dennis was a natural born entrepreneur, who became a millionaire three times over. He somehow seemed to finish up on the wrong side of the law at various times of his life. I feel sure that if he had chosen the right path, he could well have been a captain of industry. Dennis had led an amazing life. Many beautiful women, and associations with the famous and infamous.

His mother was greatly instrumental in sowing the seeds of his life into crime. She started by buying him a dinghy to use on the Regents Canal, relieving some the canal barges of their sugar cargo! He gradually developed his skills into becoming a housebreaker of large country houses! As time progressed, he was involved in all sorts of outrageous scams and fiddles. Homosexuality was illegal, at a time when he was part owner of gay night clubs in the West End of London. Dennis, I might add, was firmly heterosexual. Like many of us, he liked the good things in life. He made several earnest attempts to go straight. His first offence was for having a pistol in his car. Dennis claimed that it was placed there by a police informer; for this he was sentenced to seven years' imprisonment. He escaped from prison with an accomplice, and made his way to Newcastle. Starting a textile business with his fellow escapee within two days of arriving in Newcastle, under assumed names and knowing absolutely nothing about textiles, but his colleague did. Amazingly, the textile business thrived, even having contracts with the local police. Regretfully, he was recognised and had to leave Newcastle post-haste. Making for Southampton, he boarded a liner to the West Indies, and established yet another business! Through a girlfriend sending him a telegram, it was intercepted by the police; Scotland Yard arrived in Trinidad shortly after. That ended Dennis's idyllic life in the tropics. He was returned to England and sentenced to a further eighteen months in High-Security in Dartmoor Prison. He escaped yet again from Dartmoor with a fellow prisoner; his co-conspirator drowned in the freezing waters of a reservoir during that very daring escape. He was one of the very few prisoners to escape from Dartmoor successfully.

I had forgotten all about Dennis, only hearing from time to time that he was doing quite well running night clubs and in the slot machine business in the North East of England.

Reading a newspaper one morning, I sat bolt upright, seeing Dennis's photograph splashed across the front page. He had was been charged with the murder of an Angus Sibbet, together with a business associate named Michael Luvaglio. It became known as the "One-Armed Bandit Murder". I read the article in disbelief; an Angus Sibbett had been shot dead in his Mark X Jaguar car in the mining village of South Hetton, County Durham.

He was up to everything in the book, where there was money to be made, but I could never in a million years envisage Dennis having murdered anyone. This was at a time when the Krays and the Richardsons were rounded up and imprisoned. The strong iron fist of the law that came down was red-hot. The establishment wanted results, and managed to add another feather to its cap. He had only ever met Angus Sibbett on two occasions. No real concrete evidence, forensic evidence, or motive was ever submitted by the prosecution. Both men were confident that they would be found not guilty. They were found guilty of this crime and sentenced to life imprisonment. Whilst in prison, Dennis compiled a fifty page dossier of his case protesting his innocence; it was smuggled out to his father, who had hundreds of copies made. The dossier was sent to Members of Parliament, and people of influence who might be able to help. One was sent to an ex-girlfriend, the actress Jill Bennett, with whom he had had an affair. During their liaison, he found her to be unpredictable and highly strung. In Dennis's words, "You would certainly not take her out on a full moon!"

By this time she had married John Osborne, the playwright. Jill became influential in passing the dossier on to a writer, and Dennis's story was made into a book and a film, *Get Carter*. Carter, was the name of an old partner of Dennis's, Ken Carter. Michael Caine played Dennis in the film. Dennis was to serve twelve years in prison with his alleged accomplice; they were released on licence. He has spent forty years proclaiming his innocence and fighting for justice.

Quite naturally, he has become embittered with the justice system. "I don't want sympathy, that's something between shit and syphilis." Dennis has since co-authored a book, "The Autobiography of a Gentleman Gangster" entitled *Fun Loving Criminal*.

Leaving Barry's dance hall on a pleasant warm evening, I decided to walk back home to Bethnal Green rather than take a bus. It was a walk that took me past the Hackney Empire and the Hackney Town Hall, cutting through London Fields into The Broadway, across Hackney road and into St Peter's Avenue. This is something one would never dream of doing in the age that we are now living in, for fear of being mugged or attacked. Approaching Woolworths, in Mare Street, I encountered a well-known East End figure, Tommy Smithson. We stopped and chatted for a while. I looked for a cigarette and discovered that I had run out of them. Tommy pulled out a packet of Players that held a solitary cigarette and gave it to me. He had been a former fairground prizefighter, a merchant seaman, and somehow in his short-lived and chequered career, became a gangster. He was known in the underworld as "Mr Loser". He became a minder, working for some of the most notorious names in the criminal world, Billy Hill, Jack Coma (aka Jack Spot), and also protecting numerous Maltese club owners in the West End of London. Through his undesirable line of work it was not unusual to find his name mentioned in a newspaper for being involved in some fracas with rivals. One notable fight was with Frederick "Slim" Sullivan, resulting in Tommy slashing Slims throat and arms. He

261

had a girlfriend, Fay Richardson, a prostitute, who was
on remand for passing fraudulent cheques. Her three
former boyfriends were all murdered. This should have
been an omen for Tommy. He attempted to raise money
for her defence by calling on several of the club owners
he protected. Retaliation came his way when a meeting
was arranged for him at the Black Cap pub in Camden
Town. It was a set up! His enemies were waiting for
him, and, at a given signal, the stubbing out of a cigar,
he was attacked! He was slashed in the face, arms, and
body, in the shape of large "V"s, for vengeance; his face
required forty seven stitches. He was pushed over a wall
in Regent's Park and left for dead! However, the hard,
resilient Tommy pulled through, and it was not long
before he was again back in business. On 25 June 1950,
he went to call on George Caruana, a Maltese club
owner. A pedestrian found him lying in the gutter; he
had been shot in the neck and arms. He looked up at
the man and said, "Good morning, I'm dying!" Tommy
was thirty-six years old. On many occasions, it has been
put to me, how did I associate with these people? I
grew up with them, and knew them, as I did any other
ordinary boy or girl in the locality. They were
completely at ease in my company, because knowing
me most of my life, I was never a threat, nor did they
have to look over their shoulder in my presence. East
Enders have always held an admiration for the gangster
and the villain. The Kray twins became icons, but one
thing must be said; they never killed or maimed
innocent people. It was with their own kind and
everything was kept "in house". What I found

262

intriguing with the Kray twins, Dennis Stafford and Tommy Smithson, with the exception of Dennis who I never heard use an obscene word, was that the others could swear like troopers, yet, in the presence of elderly people, they would never allow anyone to use a bad word. They held a great respect for the aged!

From Barry's, I met up with one of the boys in the Merchant Navy. He used to come home, and tell me about his trips to Hong Kong which intrigued me. He had a very lovely sister who looked like Juliet Prowse and before long we started dating. Her brother, Derek, often suggested I should join the Merchant Navy; my other friend, Terry, kept mentioning the same thing. At that stage in life, it still concerned me that I did not know where I was going. I had no solid plans for the future and felt that I was in limbo. Thinking over my Merchant Navy friends' suggestions of joining. Initially felt a little scared that I would not be suitable. All sorts of things were racing through my mind, until I finally decided to take the plunge and apply.

The romance with this lovely girl continued and I really cared for her, but thoughts of settling down without any prospects started to give me doubts, and I became more confused, trying to work out what I really wanted in life. Should I settle into a fairly ordinary humdrum existence, remaining in the East End, or take up the opportunity to see the world? I decided to place my thoughts on hold, and see what transpired.

I applied by letter to the Peninsular & Oriental Steamship Company, 122 Leadenhall Street, in the City of London. To my surprise, I had a reply within days, asking me along for an interview and a medical. I managed to leave early in the afternoon, and raced straight from the building in which we were working in Kensington, directly to P & O's city offices. The interview went well until the medical; dropping my trousers I discovered, to my horror, that the dust and dirt from the work had penetrated them, so my legs had more dust on them than the furniture we had been shifting! I was terribly embarrassed, but with good grace, the doctor chose to ignore my discomfort. However, he discovered that I had a hernia. I practically flew off the examination table on hearing this, "No, no, it can't be me!," but it was. I was told to have an operation, then reapply to the company three months after surgery. I started cursing Foster's for all that heavy furniture we had carried up those floors at Charles House. I recalled how I used to come home with a great pain in my groin, having my grandfather to check it for me, but he had found nothing of consequence. I chose, therefore, to forget about it, when the pain wasn't so bad.

Making all the necessary arrangements via doctors and the London Hospital, I was sent to the London Hospital Annexes in Brentwood for surgery. This was to be my baptism into having "the knife". Techniques then were quite different to now, as surgery has advanced enormously. To be shaved in the nether regions by a pretty young nurse prior to surgery, I found most embarrassing! However, after a little while, you became accustomed to those procedures and took it all in your stride! During my hospital stay, the King died. It quite saddened me, hearing the news of the loss of our monarch. The other patients in the ward were affected in the same way as I; the ward suddenly developed an air of gloom for a day or so.

My girlfriend came to the hospital to visit me, she was a very caring girl. Indeed, she had also visited my grandparents, unbeknown to me. I began to feel the pressure of the situation, and the knot was beginning to tighten. I had become intrigued with one of the nurses, not romantically, of course, but she had the loveliest voice which I found absolutely enchanting. When she asked me what I would like to eat, it was as though she was singing it! Her pronunciation of the word "pudding" was like music to my ears! I became enraptured with her voice. It was even a pleasure having her take my stitches out and to listen to her speak. It was not the everyday voice you heard in the East End but I never knew where she came from. My total stay in hospital was ten days; nowadays, you would have been up and out the day following surgery.

Returning to London, I began to suffer from what I think was post-operational depression, though at the time I was completely unaware of what was happening to me. I was no longer interested in having a romantic relationship, neither did I feel amorous towards my girlfriend, and I could not understand the reasons for my "out of character behavior". Gradually, I began to ease out of the relationship, regretting to this day that I had been unable to express myself clearly to her and the reasons why I was distancing myself. I know that she was deeply hurt by my actions; it is something I have always wished I could have made amends for, but regretfully, at that time, I was not capable, and never knew how to explain my irrational behaviour.

With surgery preventing me from lifting anything, I was in no position to return to Foster's. I had to lead a fairly quiet existence for the next three months, until it was time to reapply to the P & O Shipping Company. Meanwhile, not being able to afford to be out of work, I started scanning the situations vacant columns in the London evening papers and the *Hackney Gazette* for a suitable position. As good fortune would have it, I saw a job that suited me "down to the ground". It was for a clerical position with the Royal Engineers Territorials in Victoria Park Square, advertising for a temporary "Z" callup clerk. As I had already experienced a "Z" call-up, I applied for the position and was successful.

It was a nice place to work, within easy walking distance from home, and of course being ex-army, all the army terminology was familiar to me. There were two of us in the office, plus an adjutant with his own office, who was a regular serving soldier. The hours were quite civilised and the work enjoyable in that, as I was a civilian working within a military framework, I was holding a position where I could not be disciplined for any reason! This I found encouraging, and after my army days of regimentation, very gratifying.

Our days were spent programming and sending out notices to ex-army personnel, who were subject to a "Z" call-up, which was to take place at Perranporth in Cornwall. The day arrived when we were all transported to an army barracks in Perranporth, for a

266

glorious few weeks of a wonderful summer. I was given NCO Sergeant status, both in living accommodation and messing; also the salary had all kinds of additions and perks that made it a good financial working holiday. The evenings were spent in the Sergeants' mess, with a glass in your hand, and a sing-song around a piano. Some nights we went dancing at the Blue Lagoon in Newquay. There was an RAF camp close by. Lots of service people would be in Newquay at the weekend. I recall meeting a delightful Royal Air Force "WAAF". Its funny how some names never escape you. She had the lovely name of Jean de Gruchy. We walked and talked along the sands of Newquay, sitting on the rocks, getting drenched exploring a cave, a lovely pleasant, innocent interlude. After frequently meeting on those beautiful summer evenings, we exchanged addresses and telephone numbers but our very brief encounter never developed into anything further.

Life in the barracks for that short period was great fun, working and meeting people from all walks of life, and the general camaraderie of it all. Being back in a military atmosphere, I never realised until then how much the army had indoctrinated me. Walking along the side of a road one day in the confines of the camp, a squad of soldiers came marching past, accompanied by a military band. As it was passing and without my being aware, I immediately found myself standing to attention, arms placed firmly at my side. I suddenly become conscious of my posture, and felt rather stupid! I further found that whenever a military band played, I would automatically stand shoulders back, chest out,

267

stomach in, almost marching in step to the music! The days in Perranporth waltzed by, and before we knew it, we were back in the Territorials office in Bethnal Green. The remaining weeks were spent ironing out a million and one discrepancies over non-payments and allowances that army personnel should have obtained, but hadn't up until then. The authorities concerned in providing money to families were very slow to act. This resulted in a lot of anger and frustrations, and we were left to make the apologies and attempt, as best we could, to pacify the several visits per day, mainly from wives questioning the payments that were due to them. One morning, after interviewing a host of angry people, a man walked into our office. I immediately thought it was another complaint over non-payment, but I was wrong. He introduced himself as representing Sir Alexander Korda, the filmmaker. Immediately, I became interested, and found that he was keen for the unit to provide soldiers for a film about to be made, called *Folly to be Wise* starring Alistair Sim, Elizabeth Allen and Matita Hunt. What a beautiful diversion, I thought, from handling complaints!

Approaching the adjutant concerning Sir Alexandr Korda's request, the matter was discussed and duly approved, subject to the nod from the individuals, whom I firmly believed we would have no problem with. I was correct, and every person we contacted was more than willing to participate in becoming a film extra. The pay at that time was £10 per day. This was as much as people were getting for a week's work, so quite naturally, everyone jumped at the chance, including me! I obtained permission from the adjutant to go filming along with the others.

Filming as an extra was a whole new exciting experience: being on a film lot, seeing and speaking to the stars. Alistair Sim was a pleasant man who spent some time talking with us. He was brilliant in his acting, rarely did they have to do a retake when he was before a camera. As extras, we were required to be in a small army garrison theatre, shouting and applauding at a panel of dignitaries on the stage, played by the three main stars, as well some other unknowns.

The takes and retakes went on for a few days, so we were quite delighted! Getting £10 per day was rather nice, and we wished it would never end! They were also filming on another set, *Gilbert & Sullivan*. It was rather odd seeing people walking around the studios in wigs and gowns, smoking. It seemed so out of place! Eventually, with sorrow, the filming ended and it was back to the office in Victoria Park Square. My appointment was also coming to an end, as it was almost three months since I had had the operation.

I reapplied to Peninsular & Oriental Shipping Company who, in return, requested another medical. Going though the medical examination procedures yet again, I was over the moon and jubilant to find that I had been passed fit for service! I was engaged as a "U/S" (Utility Steward) and placed on "stand-by" for the SS *Strathmore*. P & O sent me along to the Shipping Federation in Dock Street, Stepney to be registered, become a member of the National Union of Seamen, and receive a Seaman's Ration Card. In 1952 we were still on rationing, the seaman's allowance being somewhat better however, than the ordinary civilians' allowance.

A week or so passed by before I received a telegram, asking me to join the S.S. *Maloja* in King George V Dock. I packed my suitcase and bade my adieus to my grandparents; to them it was like I was going to the ends of the earth! I walked up the ship's gangway into a career that would span the next four decades. At long last, I had found my vocation; it was the sea.

That little old lady, Emma, who had helped in my mother's café and read my fortune from the tea leaves in my teacup so many years before, had been absolutely correct in her predictions. I was to travel the world many times over, and in doing so, it was to give me the greatest social education of my entire life.